conjoint family therapy

SCIENCE AND BEHAVIOR BOOKS
OF RELATED INTEREST

Family Therapy and Disturbed Families, edited by Gerald H. Zuk & Ivan Boszormenyi-Nagy

Family Dynamics and Female Sexual Delinquency, edited by Otto Pollak & Alfred S. Friedman

Communication, Family, and Marriage, edited by Don D. Jackson

An Anthology of Human Communication, 2-hour tape and companion text by Paul Watzlawick

Research in Family Interaction, edited by William D. Winter & Antonio J. Ferreira

revised edition

conjoint family therapy

*a guide
to theory
and technique*

virginia satir

formerly
Director of Training
Family Project
Mental Research Institute
Palo Alto, California

 SCIENCE AND BEHAVIOR BOOKS, INC.
PALO ALTO, CALIFORNIA

CONJOINT FAMILY THERAPY
Revised Edition

Library of Congress Card Number 67-27269

Standard Book Number 8314-0013-7

CONTENTS

FOREWORD TO THE REVISED EDITION

It has been a source of great pleasure to me to see the positive comments I made about the first edition of Mrs. Satir's book so fully borne out. More than fifteen thousand copies have been sold — a sign that many people in many professions have found this to be a useful and stimulating book.

In the period since completing this book, Mrs. Satir has traveled more miles than the Secretary of State. She is constantly searching, trying out and revising her ideas, and in this book does not attempt to detail all the new approaches she has developed. The reader may look forward to a more complete explication of the material presented in Chapter XV in a future volume.

D. D. J.

FOREWORD

It is particularly pleasurable to write the foreword to a book
that one has seen during its entire maturation process.

Virginia Satir has a well-thought-out system of conjoint family therapy that has been battle-hardened and forged in the
heat of numerous discussions with colleagues and students.
Her step-by-step approach to this system is intended as a
framework which the alert and inventive tyro will garland
with his own therapeutic devices. This detailed method offers
the student, as well as the more experienced therapist, the
opportunity to question himself about any of the manifold
situations that arise in this complicated, frustrating, exciting
form of psychotherapy.

For the theoretically minded, there is plenty to meditate
over, particularly the two chapters on communication.

Mrs. Satir is planning to follow this guidebook with a com-
plementary volume of case history material from actual therapy sessions. I am sure that this forthcoming book will throw
an even stronger beam of light on the shadowy path of family
therapy.

Don D. Jackson, M. D.
Director
Mental Research Institute
Palo Alto, California

PREFACE TO THE REVISED EDITION

The first edition of <u>Conjoint Family Therapy</u> was a long time in formulation and preparation. At times it seemed that the book would never be. Now that I have had the pleasure of authoring a book that has appealed to many people in the behavioral sciences, it is an even greater pleasure to know there is a demand for a revised edition. This is not a different book from the first edition; much of what is written there, I still believe and feel important for teaching and training. The new material, which appears primarily in Chapter XV, has been the result of the last several years' experience in traveling over the country and working with various groups, especially at the Mental Research Institute in Palo Alto and the Esalen Institute at Big Sur.

The new material is only briefly presented in this revised edition. The book I am now working on with Dr. Don D. Jackson and Dr. Arthur Bodin, of the Mental Research Institute, will contain detailed descriptions of the matters touched on in this last chapter, including clinical and training examples. To me, the most exciting development in the past several years has been the ideas, which I have shared with others and which have blossomed, dealing with the concept of growth. For too long we have been caught in the morass of "pathology" and have forgotten that growth is possible at any age, given the proper context. I continue to hope that this book will help provide a way toward that context.

V. S. S.

PREFACE

This book grew out of demands for teaching materials for a course in Family Dynamics which I taught to psychiatric residents at the Illinois State Psychiatric Institute in Chicago from 1955 to 1958. Since that time, many of my colleagues from the fields of medicine, psychiatry, psychology, social work, nursing, education, anthropology and sociology have expressed interest in my training programs in family therapy and have encouraged me to expand my initial training outlines and put them in book form. This book is the result, and represents the conclusions I have reached to date on the difficult and challenging subject of conjoint family therapy.

Many major contributions have been made to the use of the family as a therapeutic unit by people who saw behavior as a result of interactional experience in addition to intra-psychic forces. I was one of many who experimented with observing the person labeled "schizophrenic" in the presence of his family, rather than by individual treatment alone.

The germ of my particular theory and practice grew out of a new appraisal of the meaning of relatives' calls to me about the "patient" I was seeing. These calls were ostensibly in the form of complaints about the patient, or about my handling, or reports about things they thought I should know about. In traditional psychotherapeutic practice, I had been taught to view any attempt by a relative to communicate with the therapist as a potentially dangerous obstacle to the treatment relationship. As I began to try to understand the meaning of these calls, I saw that there were at least two messages conveyed in them: one about the pain or trouble that the relative observed in the patient, and one about the pain and trouble in himself.

The next step was to see that the call not only contained an offer of help to the patient, but also a request for help for the relative. It was then impossible not to recognize that there was an essential relation-

ship between a patient and his family. Any individual's behavior is a
response to the complex set of regular and predictable "rules" govern-
ing his family group, though these rules may not be consciously known
to him or the family. From this point of view, we can begin to stop
seeing relatives' activities only as dangers, and look at them as forces
for growth and indications of the power of interactional transactions.

This book is primarily intended to prepare students for effective family therapy work. For this reason, I kept the informal outline format
of the training manual from which the book originated. However,
family therapy is an area still largely unexplored, and I hope that the
book may also serve as a catalyst for innovations in both clinical practice and research.

Virginia S. Satir

ACKNOWLEDGMENTS

No man develops by himself. The evolution of this book and the ideas contained therein present a concrete example of this fact. Therefore, to all persons with whom I have had the experience of an interaction throughout my lifetime, I extend thanks for the enrichment they have given me. In particular, I cite the following:

For the encouragement I received while teaching at the Illinois State Psychiatric Institute, Chicago, Illinois, I should like to thank Dr. Kalman Gyarfas, then Director of the Institute, and Miss Pauline Peters, Director of Social Work at Chicago State Hospital, where the newly formed Institute was then housed.

My original ideas have been greatly expanded and altered through my intimate professional association with Dr. Don Jackson, Gregory Bateson, Jay Haley, John Weakland, Dr. William Fry, Dr. Jules Riskin, Dr. Robert Spitzer, and others at the Mental Research Institute, Palo Alto, California.

To my many other colleagues, now also engaged in the exciting work of studying family interaction and its relationship to the development of health and illness, I wish to express my appreciation for their willingness to offer me the findings of their research. Among these many persons are: Dr. Murray Bowen, Dr. Warren Brodey, Dr. Victor Freeman, Dr. S. Minuchin, Dr. E. Auerswald, Dr. Otto Pollak, Dr. Eric Berne, and Dr. S. I. Hayakawa.

Opportunities for clarification of my thinking have been many and rich through the questions of people who have elected to be in my training seminars or who have invited me as a consultant all over the United States. To the persons who have sought my treatment services during the past twenty-three years, I wish to extend special thanks. Without them, I would have had no way of knowing whether my ideas had any particular relevance.

I am grateful to Basic Books, New York, for permission to quote from
Murray Bowen's article, "A Family Concept of Schizophrenia," in
The Etiology of Schizophrenia, Don D. Jackson (Ed.), 1960; The Free
Press, Glencoe, Illinois, for permission to quote from "The Emotion-
ally Disturbed Child as the Family Scapegoat," by Ezra F. Vogel and
Norman W. Bell, in The Family, Bell and Vogel (Eds.), 1960; and to
International Universities Press, New York, for permission to quote
from Dr. Nathan Ackerman's article, "Behavior Trends and Disturb-
ances of the Contemporary Family," in The Family in Contemporary
Society, Iago Galdston (Ed.), 1958.

In addition, I should like to acknowledge the generous financial help
given me by the following foundations: the National Institute of Mental
Health for their Small Grant and Training Grant; Mrs. H. L. McIntyre
for her gift from the Robert C. Wheeler Foundation, and the Louis
W. and Maud Hill Family Foundation for their grant to the Family
Project.

Finally, this book would never have come into being without the able
assistance of Barbara Francisco, who spent many hours over a two
year period listening to tapes of my teaching and treatment sessions
in order to pull the material together. To Lynn Hoffman, who lent her
excellent editorial skills to putting the manuscript in its final form,
and to Camille Ball, who volunteered her help in typing the manuscript,
I give special thanks.

*   *   *   *   *   *

Since the original publication of this book, I have traveled widely and
shared experiences with many people. My thanks to all of them, and
particularly to Ruth Topping, Fritz Perls, Michael Murphy, Richard
Price and Arthur Bodin. I wish also to thank Dee Barlow Krueger for
her contribution to the preparation and writing of the Revised Edition.

*   *   *   *   *   *

KEY TO ABBREVIATIONS

Note: The following abbreviations have been used throughout the text.

I. P.	- Identified Patient	F	- Father
Th	- Therapist	M	- Mother
H	- Husband	S	- Son
W	- Wife	D	- Daughter

PART ONE: FAMILY THEORY

Chapter I

Why Family Therapy?

1. Family therapists deal with family pain.

    a. When one person in a family (the patient) has pain which shows up in symptoms, all family members are feeling this pain in some way.
    b. Many therapists have found it useful to call the member who carries the symptom the "Identified Patient," or "I.P.," rather than to join the family in calling him "the sick one," or "the different one," or "the one who is to blame."
    c. This is because the therapist sees the Identified Patient's symptoms as serving a family function as well as an individual function.

2. Numerous studies have shown that the family behaves as if it were a unit. In 1954 Jackson introduced the term "family homeostasis" to refer to this behavior. (142)

    a. According to the concept of family homeostasis, the family acts so as to achieve a balance in relationships.
    b. Members help to maintain this balance overtly and covertly.
    c. The family's repetitious, circular, predictable communication patterns reveal this balance.
    d. When the family homeostasis is precarious, members exert much effort to maintain it.

3. The marital relationship influences the character of family homeostasis.

    a. The marital relationship is the axis around which all other family relationships are formed. The mates are the "architects" of the family.

1

    b. A pained marital relationship tends to produce dysfunctional parenting.

4. The Identified Patient is the family member who is most obviously affected by the pained marital relationship and most subjected to dysfunctional parenting.

    a. His symptoms are an "SOS" about his parents' pain and the resulting family imbalance.

    b. His symptoms are a message that he is distorting his own growth as a result of trying to alleviate and absorb his parents' pain.

5. Many treatment approaches are called "family therapy" but differ from the definition which will be presented here, since they are oriented primarily to family members as individuals rather than to the family as a unit as well. For example:

    a. Each family member may have his own therapist.

    b. Or family members may share the same therapist, but the therapist sees each member separately.

    c. Or the patient may have a therapist who occasionally sees other family members "for the sake of" the patient.

6. A growing body of clinical observation has pointed to the conclusion that family therapy must be oriented to the family as a whole. This conviction was initially supported by observations showing how family members respond to the individual treatment of a family member labeled as "schizophrenic." But further studies showed that families with a delinquent member respond in similar ways to the individual treatment of this member. In both cases it was found that:

    a. Other family members interfered with, tried to become part of, or sabotaged the individual treatment of the "sick" member, as though the family had a stake in his sickness.

    b. The hospitalized or incarcerated patient often got worse or regressed after a visit from.family members, as though family interaction had a direct bearing on his symptoms.

    c. Other family members got worse as the patient got better, as though sickness in one of the family members were essential to the family's way of operating.

7. These observations led many individually-oriented psychiatrists and researchers to re-evaluate and question certain assumptions.

(109, 110, 114, 140, 142, 146, 162)

a They noted that when the patient was seen as the victim of his family, it was easy to overidentify with and overprotect him, overlooking the fact that:
-- Patients are equally adept at victimizing other family members in return.
-- Patients help to perpetuate their role as the sick, different, or blamed one.

b. They noted how heavily transference was relied on in order to produce change.
-- Yet perhaps much of the patient's so-called transference was really an appropriate reaction to the therapist's behavior in the unreal, noninteractive, therapeutic situation.
-- In addition, there was a greater chance that the therapeutic situation would perpetuate pathology, instead of presenting a new state of affairs which would introduce doubts about the old perceptions.
-- If some of the patient's behavior did represent transference (that is, his characteristic way of relating to his mother and father), why shouldn't the therapist help the patient deal with the family more directly, by seeing both the patient and his family together?

c. They noted that the therapist tended to be more interested in the patient's fantasy life than in his real life. But even if they were interested in the patient's real life, as long as they saw just the patient in therapy, they had to rely on his version of that life or try and guess what was going on in it.

d. They noted that in trying to change one family member's way of operating they were, in effect, trying to change the whole family's way of operating.
-- This put the burden of family change-agent on the patient all by himself rather than on all family members.
-- The patient was already the family member who was trying to change the family's way of operating, so when he was urged to increase his efforts, he only received a more intense criticism from the family. This also led him to feel even more burdened and less able.

8. Aside from all these observations, once therapists started to see the whole family together, other aspects of family life which produced symptoms were revealed, aspects which had been largely overlooked. Other investigators of family interaction were making similar discoveries. As Warren Brodey sees it, the mates act differently with the normal sibling than they do with the symptomatic sibling:

...the parents in the presence of the "normal" sibling are able to relate with a freedom, flexibility, and breadth of awareness that one finds hard to believe, considering the limitations that exist in the relationship between the parents when involved with the symptomatic sibling. The pathological ways of relating seem to be focused within the relationship with the symptomatic member. One wonders how this has come about. *

9. But those psychiatrists who became increasingly devoted to family therapy were not the first to recognize the interpersonal nature of mental illness. Sullivan and Fromm-Reichmann, along with many other psychiatrists, psychologists, and social workers, were pioneers in this area of discovery. The Child Guidance movement was another important development which helped break the tradition of singling out just one family member for treatment. (159)

   a. Child Guidance therapists included both mother and child in treatment, even though they still tended to see mother and child in separate treatment sessions.
   b. They also increasingly recognized the importance of including the father in therapy, though they found him hard to reach, and generally failed to engage him in the therapy process.
      -- Therapists reported that the father felt parenting was his wife's job more than his; if the child acted disturbed, his wife was the one who should be seen.
      -- The Child Guidance therapists, being mother-child oriented anyway, tended to agree with the father's reasoning, so they could not easily convince him that his role in the family was important to the health of his child.
      -- Child Guidance Clinics remained primarily focused on "mothering," even though they increasingly recognized the importance of "fathering." And whether or not they included the father in their thinking, they continued to focus on the husband and wife as parents of the child rather than as mates to each other. Yet it has been repeatedly noted how critically the marital relationship affects parenting. Murray Bowen writes, for example:

         The striking observation was that when the parents were emotionally close, more invested in each other than either was in the patient, the patient improved.

---

*Murray Bowen. A family concept of schizophrenia. In Don D. Jackson (Ed.), *The Etiology of Schizophrenia*. New York: Basic Books, 1960; p.370.

When <u>either</u> parent became more emotionally invested in the patient than in the other parent, the patient immediately and automatically regressed. When the parents were emotionally close, they could do no wrong in their "management" of the patient. The patient responded well to firmness, permissiveness, punishment, "talking it out," or any other management approach. When the parents were "emotionally divorced," any and all "management approaches" were equally unsuccessful. *

10. Family therapists have found it easier to interest the husband in family therapy than in individual therapy. This is because the family therapist is himself convinced that both architects of the family must be present.

   a. Once the therapist convinces the husband that he is essential to the therapy process, and that no one else can speak for him or take his place in therapy <u>or</u> in family life, he readily enters in.
   b. The wife (in her role as mother) may initiate family therapy, but once therapy is under way, the husband becomes as involved as she does.
   c. Family therapy seems to make sense to the whole family. Husband and wife say: "Now, at last, we are together and can get to the bottom of this."

11. Right from the first contact, family therapists operate from certain assumptions about why a family member has sought therapeutic help.

   a. Usually the first contact is made because someone outside the family has labeled Johnny as disturbed. This first contact will probably be made by an anxious wife (we will call her Mary Jones), acting in her role as mother of a disturbed child, Johnny. The child is disturbed, so she, the mother, must be to blame.
   b. But Johnny was probably exhibiting disturbed behavior long before he became labeled disturbed by someone outside the family.
   c. Until the outsider (often a teacher) labeled Johnny as disturbed, members of the Jones family probably acted as though they did

*W.M. Brodey Some family operations of schizophrenia: a study of five hospitalized families each with a schizophrenic member. Arch. gen. Psychiat., 1: 379-402, 1959; p.391

not notice Johnny's behavior; his behavior was appropriate because it served a family function.

d. Usually some event has occurred which has precipitated symptoms in Johnny, symptoms which make the fact that he is disturbed obvious to outsiders. These events are:
-- Changes from outside the nuclear family: war, depression, etc.
-- Changes in the two families of origin: sickness of a grandmother, financial distress of a grandfather, etc.
-- Someone enters or leaves the nuclear family: grandmother comes to live with the family, the family takes on a boarder, the family adds to its membership with the birth of another child, a daughter gets married.
-- Biological changes: a child reaches adolescence, mother reaches menopause, father is hospitalized.
-- Major social changes: a child leaves home to attend school, the family moves to a new neighborhood, father gets a job promotion, son goes to college.

e. These events can precipitate symptoms because they require the mates to integrate the changes. This requirement puts an extra strain on the marital relationship because it calls for a redefinition of family relationships and thus affects family balance.

f. The family homeostasis can be functional (or "fitting") for members at some periods of family life and not at other periods, so events affect members differently at different times.

g. But if one member is affected by an event, all are to some degree.

12. After the first contact with Mary Jones, the therapist may speculate about the relationship between Mary and her husband, whom we will call Joe. If it is correct to assume that a dysfunctional marital relationship is the main contributor to symptoms in a child, the relationship between the mates will be the therapist's first concern.

a. What kind of people are Mary and Joe? What kind of families did they come from?
-- Once they were two separate people who came from different family environments.
-- Now they are the architects of a new family of their own.

b. Why, out of all the people in the world, did they choose each other as mates?
-- How they chose each other gives clues to why they may now be disappointed with each other.

-- How they express their disappointment with each other gives clues to why Johnny needs to have symptoms in order to hold the Jones family together.

Chapter II

Low Self-Esteem and Mate Selection

1. A person with low self-esteem has a great sense of anxiety and uncertainty about himself.

    a. His self-esteem is based to an extreme extent on what he thinks others think of him.
    b. His dependence on others for his self-esteem cripples his autonomy and individuality.
    c. He disguises his low self-esteem from others, especially when he wants to impress others.
    d. His low self-esteem comes from his growing-up experiences which never led him to feel that it is good to be a person of one sex in relation to a person of the other.
    e. He has never really separated from his parents, that is, arrived at a relationship of equality with them.

2. A person with low self-esteem has high hopes about what he can expect from others, but he also has great fears; he is only too ready to expect disappointment and to distrust people.

    a. When Mary and Joe enter therapy, the therapist will try to find out what they hoped for and feared from each other in their early courtship period, because:
    -- It was not an accident that they selected one another as mates; there was something they saw in each other which seemed to fit their high hopes.
    -- There was also something they saw in each other (but did not permit themselves to openly acknowledge) which seemed to corroborate their fears or distrust. The therapist will find them inducing the feared, expected behavior in the other as if they were trying to get the uncertainty over with (as if they were trying to fulfill their own prophesies).
    -- Their marital relationship will, in many respects, duplicate or be diametrically opposed to the relationship which each saw existing between his own parents.

3. Perhaps Mary and Joe each saw what he hoped for in the other because each was behaving at the level of his defenses rather than at the level of his inner feelings.

   a. Joe acted self-confident and strong on the outside but felt uncertain, helpless, and frightened on the inside. When Mary looked at Joe she could say: "Here is a strong person who can take care of me."
   b. Mary acted self-confident, outgoing, talkative on the outside but felt uncertain, helpless, frightened on the inside. When Joe looked at Mary he could say: "Here is a strong person who can take care of me."
   c. After marriage, each found the other was not the strong person for which he hoped. Frustration, disappointment, anger, were bound to result.

4. One might wonder how Mary and Joe managed to find a mate if they had such low self-esteem and so little trust.

   a. Once puberty brought adult sexuality to the fore, they risked relationship in spite of all their fears.
   b. Also, they were in love which, for the time, enhanced their self-esteem and made each feel complete. Each said: "You seem to value me...I am lucky to have you...I need you in order to survive...I am complete if you are around."
   c. Both ended up living for each other and, in doing so, entered into a "survival pact." Each said privately to himself: "If I run out of supplies I will take from you. You will have enough, in an emergency, to serve us both."

5. The trouble was, when choosing each other as mates, that Mary and Joe did not communicate their fears to each other.

   a. Joe feared that Mary would not love him if she knew about his worthlessness (and vice versa).
      -- It was as if Joe said privately to himself: "I must not reveal that I am nothing. Nor must I reveal the fact that I secretly expect all women to be unfair, irrational, sarcastic, stubborn, domineering. I must not reveal my belief that the only way to survive with a woman is to withdraw from the scene and let her run the show."
      -- It was as if Mary said privately to herself: "I must not reveal that I am nothing. Nor must I reveal that I secretly expect all men to be stingy, irresponsible, indecisive, weak, and let women carry the burden. I must not reveal

my belief that the only way to survive with a man is to be ready to shoulder the burden the minute he complains. "

b. Yet in spite of what each privately expected from the other and thought of himself, each also felt he must be what he thought the other saw in him because he had put the other in charge of his self-esteem.

-- When Mary let Joe know that she saw him as strong, Joe at first saw Mary's perception as strengthening; he could feel strong because she saw him as strong (and vice versa).

-- This kind of relationship can be maintained until an environmental stress or a decision-making requirement challenges Mary and Joe's ability to cope. Only then does strength begin to look like a cover-up for weakness or like domination.

c. Neither Mary nor Joe can ask what the other expects, hopes for, fears, because both feel they are supposed to be able to guess about what is going on inside the other's skin. (In other words, it is as if both live by a crystal ball.)

d. Since each operates from the assumption that he must please the other, neither of them can communicate when he is displeased with the other, or acknowledge disagreement or criticism directly. They operate as though they must be indistinguishable from each other. They live as though they were on the same bloodstream, on the same survival pipeline. For example, I once had a marital pair who sat at the therapy table throughout the first two sessions with their arms intertwined, while their child, experiencing the tragedy of it all, sat across from them hallucinating.

6. In effect, Mary and Joe married to "get."

a. Each wanted the other's esteem of him. (Both also wanted society's esteem of them: "One should get married. I have now succeeded.")

b. Each wanted the other's qualities which he felt he lacked (qualities which he tried to make a part of himself).

c. Each wanted an extension of himself.

d. Each wanted an omnipotent, omniscient, selfless, "good" parent in the other, and wanted to avoid the omniscient, omnipotent "bad" parent.

Chapter III

Different-ness and Disagreements

1. When Mary and Joe married they did not realize that they would have to "give" as well as get.

   a. Each felt he had nothing to give.
   b. Each felt he should not be expected to give because the other was an extension of the self.
   c. If either did give, he did so grudgingly or anxiously or self-sacrificingly because neither really expected to get.

2. When Mary and Joe discover, after marriage, that the other is "different" from what each expected during courtship, they become disillusioned. What they actually now see in the other are the twenty-four-hour-a-day characteristics which do not usually show up during courtship, and consequently do not fit their expectations.

   a. Mary puts her hair in curlers when she goes to bed at night.
   b. Mary persistently serves overcooked beans.
   c. Joe leaves his dirty socks strewn around the room.
   d. When Joe goes to bed at night he snores.

3. When Mary and Joe discover, after marriage, that they are different in ways which seem to take away rather than add to them, they see each other in a new light.

   a. "Different-ness" looks bad because it leads to disagreement.
   b. Disagreement reminds them both that the other is not an extension of the self but is separate.

4. I mean the term "different-ness" to cover the whole area of individuality, how each person is innately different from every other person.

   a. People can be physically different (A is tall, B short; A is male, B female).

11

    b. People can have different personalities or temperament (A is excitable and outgoing, B placid and reserved).

    c. People can have different educational backgrounds and abilities (A knows about physics, B about music; A has good tool dexterity, B can sing).

    d. The presence of different-ness in another can be used destructively, rather than as an opportunity for enrichment.

5. The particular kinds of different-ness which bother Mary and Joe the most are:

    a. Different preferences, wishes, habits, tastes (A likes to go fishing, B hates it; A likes the window open at night, B likes it closed).

    b. Different expectations and opinions (A expects women to be strong, B expects men to be strong; A has religious convictions, B doesn't).

6. Different-ness which leads to a conflict of interests (disagreement) is seen as an insult and as evidence of being unloved.

    a. It seems to threaten autonomy and self-esteem.

    b. One may have to give while the other gets. Yet there isn't enough to go around. Who will get what is available?

    c. Before marriage, each thought the other had enough for two people. Now, when disagreement comes up, it looks as if there may not even be enough for one.

7. If Mary and Joe had self-esteem, each would be able to trust the other.

    a. Each would feel confident in his ability to get from the other.

    b. Each could even wait to get.

    c. Each could give to the other without himself feeling robbed.

    d. Each could use the different-ness of the other as an opportunity for growth.

8. Mary and Joe lack trust.

    a. Each feels he has barely enough to sustain his own life, let alone the other's life.

    b. Each behaves as if he were saying: "I am nothing. I will live for you." But each also behaves as if he were saying: "I am nothing, so please live for me."

9. Because they lack trust, certain areas of joint living which especially challenge their ability to take into account the individuality of the other are especially threatening to them. These areas
are: money, food, sex, recreation, work, child-rearing, relations with in-laws.

10. Even if they were able to trust others, joint living forces on them
decisions about when to give, when to get, within the context of
reality at the time. They must decide:

   a. What they will share or do together (how dependent they will
   be).
   b. What they will not share or do separately (how independent
   they will be).

11. They must strike some kind of balance within the current reality
as to:

   a. What A wants and what B wants.
   b. What A does best and B does best.
   c. What A thinks and what B thinks.
   d. How A will carry responsibilities and how B will carry responsibilities.

12. They need to learn how to assert their thoughts, wishes, feelings
and knowledge without destroying, invading or obliterating the
other, and while still coming out with a fitting joint outcome.

   a. If they are able to work out a functional relationship, they will
   say: "I think what I think, feel what I feel, know what I know. I
   am being me, but I do not blame you for being you. I welcome
   what you have to offer. Let us both see what we can work out
   that would be most realistic."
   b. But if they are not able to work out a functional relationship,
   they will say: "Be like me; be one with me. You are bad if you
   disagree with me. Reality and your different-ness are unimportant."

13. Let us take a trivial example of how "functional" people disagree.
Let us say that a couple already understands and accepts the fact
that it would be nice to have dinner together. But we will also say
that A wants to go out for a hamburger dinner and B wants to go
out for a chicken dinner. The place which serves hamburger does
not serve chicken; the place which serves chicken does not serve
hamburger.

a. Each may try to coax: "Please eat hamburgers."
b. Each may try taking turns: "Let's eat chicken this time and hamburger next time."
c. They may try to find an alternative which pleases both: "We both like steak so let's eat steak" or "Let's find another restaurant which serves hamburger and chicken."
d. They may take into account a realistic concern which outweighs their separate wishes: "Since the hamburger place is nearer, and we're in a hurry, let's eat hamburger."
e. They may try to balance their separate wishes against their wish to be together: "You eat hamburger since you like it so much and I will eat chicken, and I will see you later." They are able to separate temporarily and find independent solutions when independence is feasible.
f. As a last-ditch effort, they may use a third person to make the decision for them: "Charlie wants to eat with us. Let's ask Charlie where he wants to go."

14. Let us take the same example and see how "dysfunctional" people disagree. They operate from the principle that love and total agreement go together. Therefore:

a. We find them vacillating and postponing: "Let's decide later what to eat" (and they sometimes skip the meal altogether).
b. We find them trying to coerce: "We are going to eat hamburgers!"
c. We find them trying to delude each other: "They are both food, so let's eat hamburger."
d. We find them trying to undermine each other: "You don't really like chicken" or, "you must be crazy to like chicken."
e. Always we find them accusing and evaluating morally: "You are bad and selfish for not wanting to eat hamburger. You never do what I want. You have mean intentions toward me."

15. Mary and Joe, to the degree that they are dysfunctional, in effect disagree by saying: "If you loved me you would do what I want." They never use the technique of separating and finding independent solutions; agreed-upon independence is never feasible.

16. Mary and Joe accuse each other because they are disappointed and hurt; they expected total agreement.

a. They expected to be valued by the other and they see themselves getting accusations instead.

b. They expected to be one with the other and they see themselves getting separation and different-ness instead.

17. Yet if Mary and Joe accuse too openly, several dire results are expected. Joe behaves as if he had said privately to himself:

"If I accuse Mary, Mary will fall apart. I can't let Mary fall apart because I need her to value me. And suppose Mary refuses to fall apart because she really does not value me? Suppose, instead, that Mary accuses me, hurts me, casts me back into separateness and psychological death, causes me to fall apart?"

"No, that must not happen! Mary needs me. I am responsible for her. I must not accuse Mary or she will fall apart. If I do accuse, I must do it very carefully."

Mary does the same.

18. The disagreement process between Mary and Joe must go underground. (As a matter of fact, most of their communication goes underground, i.e., becomes covert.)

a. When Joe and Mary want to accuse each other for not giving, they must hide their accusation and thus communicate covertly.
b. When they want to ask for something, they must hide their asking and thus communicate covertly.

19. Here is an example of what covert asking sounds like. Let's say Mary wants to see a movie.

a. Instead of Mary saying, "I want to see a movie. Do you?" she may say to Joe, "You would like to see a movie, wouldn't you?" or, "It would do you good to see a movie."
b. If she has to hide her request even more (if, for example, she is what we call "schizophrenic"), she may say, "There's a new movie house down the street" or, "I like air conditioning."

20. Here is an example of what covert accusation sounds like. Suppose that Joe does not respond to Mary's request.

a. Instead of Mary saying, "You don't hear me when I ask for something. You are a schmo!" Mary says, "People never pay attention to me."
b. Or, if she has to hide her accusation even more (as with the

schizophrenic), she may say, "The world has no ears."

21. When asking and accusing become this hidden, any third person looking on becomes confused and asks: "Who wants what from whom? Who did what to whom?"

   a. A child in the family can become confused.
   b. A therapist can become confused unless he sees to it that wishes and accusations get clearly labeled as coming from someone and going toward someone.

22. As one observes people along the continuum from most functional to least functional, wishes and accusations have fewer and fewer owners.

   a. They become addressed to the nearest planet rather than to the nearest person.
   b. Responses to requests and accusations become increasingly evasive.
      -- Messages are sent out as if to no one.
      -- Responses are also returned as if to no one.

23. Mary and Joe can evade requests and accusations by withdrawing from the situation. At the same time, they turn their overt withdrawal into a covert accusation.

   a. They may withdraw in so many words: "Do what you like... Do it your way... You, dear, are always right."
   b. They may withdraw without words by literally leaving the field during crucial decision-making periods, and doing it in such a way that they are covertly saying: "Do what you like. I have to be absent in order to live with you."
   c. They may withdraw through drugs, sleep, alcohol, inattention, "stupidity," in which case they are saying: "Do what you like. I have to be half-conscious in order to live with you."
   d. They may withdraw through physical illness, in which case they are saying: "Do what you like. I have to be sick in order to live with you."
   e. As a last resort, they may withdraw through mental illness, in which case they are saying: "Do what you like. I have to be crazy in order to live with you."

24. Beneath all the evasiveness and ambiguity, Mary and Joe are still trying to solve their conflicting feelings about whether they are loved or unloved.

a. Each is trying to cover up his disappointment.
b. Each is trying to propitiate, protect, and please the other because he needs the other in order to survive.
c. Whatever they do, the way in which they do it tells how disappointed, martyred, robbed they feel.

25. As a therapist, I have found that the more covertly and indirectly
people communicate, the more dysfunctional they are likely to be.
However, I have said nothing about the couples who pull and tug
in what I call the "teeter-totter syndrome."

a. Each says: "I'm right!" "No, I'm right!"
"You are a schmo!" "No, you are a schmo!"
b. Teeter-totter couples at least pull and tug out in the open.
-- They do not agree overtly and at the same time disagree
covertly.
-- One mate does not confuse his own wishes with the other's.
Each can hear the other's wishes quite easily because they
are usually shouting them.
-- Any third person can easily see that these two do not agree
and can also comment on this fact and have the comment
agreed with.
-- The teeter-totter man and wife do not kid themselves, each
other, or other people, about how disappointed they feel.
However, their individual feelings of low self-esteem create a mutual need for each other and they feel caught. They
can acknowledge different-ness but not separateness.

26. To summarize, Mary and Joe, if they are dysfunctional to an extreme degree (parents of a severely disturbed child), will have
low self-esteem, high hopes, and little trust. Thus, they can
easily solidify a relationship in which the self and the other become indistinguishable at the surface level. The uniqueness of
the self can only be acknowledged covertly.

a. It is as if Joe says to himself: "Mary needs me, I am responsible for her. I must not disagree with Mary, or she will fall
apart. Mary and I, we are not different. And we must show no
disagreement either except on minor things. She feels what I
feel, likes what I like, thinks what I think. We are on the same
bloodstream, we live for each other."
b. Each tries so hard to please and protect the other that he ends
up living by what he thinks the other wants of him.
-- Each gives control of himself to the other, while resenting
it.

-- Each also accepts responsibility for controlling the other, while resenting it.

27. In effect, each ends up acting like a parent one minute and a child the next.

    a. Each says: "Here, run my life for me (yet I wish you wouldn't!)
    b. Each also says: "All right, I will run your life for you (yet I wish you would run your own)."
    c. Each takes turns at being either the strong, adequate one, or the helpless, inadequate one. There is only room in the relationship for one strong, adequate person.
    d. Each operates as though being an individual and being a husband or a wife are incompatible; as though individuality and marriage don't go together.

28. Before marriage, Mary and Joe had never thoroughly manifested themselves as individuals.

    a. Now, after marriage, they try not to show what little individuality they previously manifested, in order to take on the marital role.
    b. Now, overtly, they try to be just mates living for each other.
    c. Covertly, they are still trying to exert themselves as individuals.

29. Mary and Joe continue in this kind of relationship because they really expected no other kind.

    a. They can always hope it will be different for them (Life is as life was -- but then, maybe it isn't!).
    -- Mary can hope that Joe is not what she expected in a man.
    -- Joe can hope that Mary is not what he expected in a woman.
    b. Meanwhile, Mary must defend herself against her fears by using the same tactics her parents used against each other because she knows no other kind. (Joe does the same.)

30. Whatever kind of relationship Mary and Joe have worked out, they are disappointed with what they got.

    a. Soon they will be adding the parental role to what is left of their individual roles and to what they have tried to develop as marital roles.

b. If they found it hard to integrate being an individual with being a mate, they will find it equally hard to integrate being a parent.

Chapter IV

Stresses Affecting the Modern Family

1. When Johnny enters the Jones world, his parents' expectations and needs are there to greet him.

   a. Johnny, by his very existence, offers Mary and Joe another chance to "get," another chance to feel adequate, lovable, needed, strong, complete.
   b. Johnny offers his parents a chance to get a true extension of themselves, one consisting of their own flesh and blood.

2. The trouble is, Johnny has some immediate wants of his own.

   a. Right from birth, he makes it clear that <u>he</u> is out to get, since he is physically helpless and psychologically unrelated and un-socialized.
   b. But because he is helpless, his own survival needs must be met within the framework of his parents' needs and expecta-tions. If he is going to get what he needs, his asking must be tuned to what his parents are willing and able to give.

3. When Mary and Joe added the parental role to their individual and marital roles, they then qualified, sociologically speaking, as a family. Before discussing the Jones family, it may be profitable to remind ourselves about what sociologists and anthropologists have decided families are, and what functions they perform as a crucial sub-unit of every society.

   a. They generally seem to agree that the nuclear family (made up of parents and children) is found in all societies.
   b. They define a family as a group composed of adults of both sexes, two of whom (the mates) live under the same roof and maintain a socially accepted sexual relationship.
   c. Families also include children created or adopted by these mates.

4. As a social institution, such a group of individuals is held together by mutually-reinforcing functions. These functions are:

   a. To provide a genital heterosexual experience for the mates.
   b. To contribute to the continuity of the race by producing and
nurturing children.
   c. To cooperate economically by dividing labors between the
adults according to sex, convenience, and precedents, and
between adults and children according to the child's age and
sex.
   d. To maintain a boundary (by the incest taboo) between the generations so that smooth task-functioning and stable relationships can be maintained.
   e. To transmit culture to the children by parental teaching.
     -- To teach "roles" or socially accepted ways to act with
others in different social situations. (These roles vary
according to the age and sex of the child.)
     -- To teach the child how to cope with the inanimate environ-
ment.
     -- To teach the child how to communicate; how to use words
and gestures so that they will have a generally accepted
meaning for others.
     -- To teach how and when to express emotions, generally
guiding the child's emotional reactivity. (The family teaches
the child by appealing to his love and to his fear, by communicating to him verbally, nonverbally, and by example.)
   f. To recognize when one of its members is no longer a child but
has become an adult, capable of performing adult roles and
functions.
   g. To provide for the eventual care of parents by their children.

5. This is a tall order for families, especially for the mates. Why
are mates willing to take on such obligations? Because children
are economic assets? Because children are emotional assets?
The answer to this question is culturally determined. In our culture, the emotional assets of children predominate.

   a. Joe (and the following is true for Mary, too) can feel he has
succeeded in fulfilling society's expectations: "Adults bear
children. I have a child, too."
   b. Joe can gain a feeling of perpetuity by leaving one of his own
flesh and blood to live after him.
   c. Joe can enjoy over again parts of his own past life by vicar-
iously experiencing his child's discoveries, joys, wonderment.
   d. Joe can try to correct for his past pains and mistakes by try-

ing to help his child avoid the avoidable and anticipate future problems.

e. Joe gains added purpose when he notes how very important he is to the child. He must care for, protect, guide, be responsible for his child because he, the father, is obviously the wiser one, the more accomplished one, the authority, the truly stronger one.

f. Joe can feel united with Mary, and Mary can feel united with Joe.

-- It took both mates to produce a child; neither could achieve this feat alone.

-- It will now take the joint efforts of both to nurture and educate their child; one parent cannot achieve this feat alone, either.

6. But there are deficits to parenting, too, which can fill new parents with conflicting feelings.

a. Joe and Mary may not have planned to be parents at the time when they actually conceived their child. Perhaps all they thought about were the sexual gratifications they were receiving from each other.

b. They may have been economically unready to take on responsibilities of feeding, clothing, sheltering.

-- Joe may see the child as demanding an economic support which he feels unable to supply.

-- Mary may have a job which adds to family income (and which she also enjoys), which must now be given up for the sake of the child.

c. They may be emotionally unready to add a third, dependent member and become a family.

-- Joe may see the child as diminishing Mary's interest in him.

-- Mary may see the child as diverting Joe's interest from her.

-- Mary, who by necessity will take the lion's share of early parenting, may also see the child as a creature who demands all of her and gives little in return, requiring her to isolate herself from adults all day while catering to its needs.

-- Both may be frightened by the total responsibility thrust upon them.

-- Both may wonder, now that the third member creates a family triangle, if someone won't sooner or later get left out.

7. But these are not problems which only Mary and Joe have. All families in the western world have gone through (and are still reacting to) several material and philosophical influences affecting society as a whole.

8. The Industrial Revolution profoundly affected the modern family, relieving mates of many burdens, yet also placing many extra strains upon them. The effects of this revolution are well known but bear brief repetition here:

   a. It mechanized and de-personalized the work world, leaving the male feeling like a meaningless automaton, laboring at tasks which were only a tiny part of a gigantic, incomprehensible, valueless whole.
   b. It caused individual worth to be rated by income earned, leaving the female feeling down-graded because she did not receive wages for keeping house and rearing children.
   c. Maybe she did not choose to earn her own living, but chose to stay home in the role of wife and mother. If so, she found many family functions taken over by outside institutions: education, food preparation, etc.
   d. The Industrial Revolution emphasized individual mobility as an essential condition of advancement, requiring that whole families follow the money-earner from community to community, leaving old friends behind.
   e. It helped to separate parents from grandparents while failing to replace functions which grandparents previously performed for the nuclear family (such as post-natal home care, baby-sitting, emergency financial assistance).
   f. The industrial complex made increased specialization in all areas of life mandatory, leaving the individual feeling powerless to influence outer events (local, national, and international). The outside had become a potentially dangerous source of forces which he could barely understand and over which he felt he had no control.

9. Revolutionary intellectual and social influences also affected the modern family by calling into question old assumptions, absolutes, norms, values.

   a. A person's role was no longer something automatic, unquestioned, pre-determined by a static social order and by pre-arranged manners and customs.
   b. Roles often had to be learned anew for new situations.

    c. Worth had to be earned; it did not come as a birthright. Even
if it did come by being earned, it was still uncertainly "relative. "

    d. Old patriarchal definitions of the male as the head of the house
and the female as belonging in the home went through a re-eval-
uation. Confused men and women, reacting to the new equalii-
tarian ideals, found themselves questioning and worrying about
everyday family tasks and roles.

10. Psychoanalysis, also, profoundly affected concepts about "normal" human behavior, motivation, learning. It led people to re-
examine and worry about all aspects of existence, especially
about proper child-rearing practices.

    a. The theory implicitly urged parents to give the child freedom
to avoid injuring his psychic development.

    b. Over-applied (or carried to a logical conclusion), such ideas
immobilized and confused parents. Should they spank or not
spank their child? Should they put any restraints on him whatsoever? Family life became increasingly democratic, with
children of all ages given a voice and authority about their own
upbringing.

11. All these philosophical and economic trends left males and females feeling confused and unimportant.

    a. Men's family lives became so separated from their work lives
that they lived almost in two separate worlds.
      -- In their work lives, behind a desk shuffling endless papers
or behind a machine tightening endless bolts, they felt small,
helpless, ignored, insecure.
      -- Whatever they managed to earn, their families as quickly
gobbled up.
      -- In their home lives they often. felt like mother's helper or
mother's auxiliary disciplinary force.
      -- They often wished the family would be geared more to their
needs. They were tired and discouraged and rattled from
the day's exploits and decisions. They could do with a family turned rest-home or quiet sanitarium.
      -- Sons, especially, would find an absent, preoccupied, tired,
or demoted father an uncertain figure by which to model
their lives.

    b. Women, living in cities in "boxes in the air" or tucked away
in suburbs, felt separated from the bustle and "real purpose"

of the modern-day world.

-- They had been educated for tasks other than housekeeping and child-rearing, and taught to be aware of scientific and cultural events going on outside the family world. They now found themselves losing work experience, seniority, self-confidence, as they focused solely on the wife and mother roles.

-- As they focused on housekeeping and child-rearing, society, in turn, took many of their chores away from them or made their household tasks easier and thus more quickly accomplished.

-- Some women went outside the home to work, placing their children in nurseries, with neighbors, or with a succession of babysitters. Some stayed home and fretted, parenting in a listless, half-hearted, absent-minded way. Some stayed home and turned child-rearing into an over-intense occupation to compensate for a feeling of uselessness and a feeling that life was passing them by.

12. It is not coincidental that ideas of romantic love and personal happiness became popular in western culture at the same time that old certainties about being a male, being a female, being a person, were shifting and fading.

a. When people felt like "nothing," they were all the more anxious to feel like "everything" to someone.

b. When people could choose a mate to guarantee their personal happiness, and divorce could end the relationship at will, every married day could become a shall-we-stay-in-it-or-shall-we-get-out-of-it? day.

c. When people could enter a relationship with a hypothetical, impermanent attitude, they could become so busy feeling their pulse for degrees of happiness that they had little time for enjoying a relationship.

13. Nathan Ackerman, discussing the way wider social conditions have affected the family, says:

The mark of our time is the peculiar disharmony of the individual's relations with wider society. A variety of hypotheses come to mind; Durkheim's concept of anomie, Fromm's emphasis on the trend to alienation, Riesman's theory of the other-directed man. Whatever the term, all are agreed on the trend toward a sense of lostness, aloneness, confusion of personal identity, and a driven search for acceptance through

conformity. One effect of this trend toward disorientation is
to throw each person back upon his family group for the res-
toration of a sense of security, belongingness, dignity and
worth. The family is called upon to make up to its individual
members in affection and closeness for the anxiety and distress which is the result of failure to find a safe place in the
wider world. Individuals pitch themselves back on their families for reassurance as to their lovableness and worth. This
pressure to compensate individual members with special security and affection imposes upon the family an extra psychic
load. Is the contemporary family equipped to carry this extra
load? No — not very well! The family tries, but it achieves
at best a precarious success; often it fails. *

14. Once two World Wars had further disillusioned men and women,
they turned to family-building as a total reason for being. (House-
building and baby-production boomed and still continue to boom.)

   a. Child-rearing became a major business and preoccupation of
   males and females alike.
   b. Making children happy became a major theme.
   c. Giving children what the parents never had became a necessity.
   d. A child's growth, development, and achievements became a
   major way for parents to validate their personal worth.
   e. A child's attitude toward his parents could, to a large extent,
   make or break their feelings of self-esteem.

15. The parental role took over, as males and females continued to
find their relations with each other thorny and threatening.

   a. Disillusioned with each other, they agreed to "live for the
   child."
   b. Yet they implicitly asked that the child live for them; he was
   the important one, the one who had the power, the responsibility, the mandate to make his parents happy.

*Nathan W. Ackerman. Behavior trends and disturbances of the contemporary family.
In I. Galdston (Ed.), *The Family in Contemporary Society*. New York: Int. Univ.
Press, 1958; p.57.

Chapter V

Marital Disappointment and Its Consequences for the Child

1. All modern families go through the stresses and strains of modern society. Yet some manage to produce self-confident children who are capable of coping successfully with a difficult environment.

   a. Sociologists point to delinquent neighborhoods as a major factor in producing delinquency in children. Yet many families live in these neighborhoods and do not produce delinquents, while others in the same neighborhoods produce delinquents in droves.

   b. Psychiatry generally tries to explain these different outcomes by saying that the child who becomes delinquent has a deficiency in psychic functioning: a deficiency in ego development or super-ego controls.

   c. Those of us who have studied family interaction as it affects behavior in children cannot help wondering why the therapy professions have so long overlooked the family as the critical intervening variable between the society and the individual.

   -- The family system is the main learning context for individual behavior, thoughts, feelings.

   -- How parents teach a child is just as important as what they teach.

   -- Also, since two parents are teaching the child, we must study family interaction if we are going to understand what the family learning context is like.

2. Family theory postulates that outside forces are important mainly as they affect the parents.

   a. The parents, who teach by words and by demonstration, are the ones who translate to the child the major meaning which outside forces will have to the family.

   b. If the parents, as mates, are disappointed in each other and thus feeling upset, confused, empty, despairing, any outside stress will pack an extra wallop.

c. If the mates, as individuals, did not integrate what they learned in their own families, they will find it particularly hard to work out a marital integration so that they can give clear, consistent messages to their children.

d. They will also distort or misinterpret influence from the outside in order to maintain a shaky self-esteem.

3. The marital relationship between Mary and Joe is dysfunctional. As was described, Mary and Joe are low in self-esteem. They looked to each other to enhance self-esteem. But because each saw the other as an extension of self, each failed to give to the other as well as get from the other. So their relationship only increased low feelings of self-esteem. They both became disillusioned and disappointed. The question now remains: How do they fare as parents? To answer this question, one must also ask: How do they see the child? They will see him:

a. As a vehicle for representing their worth in the community ard for maintaining esteem about self and family.

> "He is the best reader in his class."
> "Everyone says she is the best-behaved child!"
> "We wanted our kid to be what we couldn't be."

b. As a vehicle for maintaining their esteem as people and more particularly as parents. They need to feel that the child likes them.
   -- If, by the child's behavior, he shows that he disapproves of them, they are disappointed.
   -- This makes it difficult to discipline the child.

c. As an extension of the self.
   -- As wanting what they wanted when young. If he doesn't want the same things, they are disappointed.
   -- As thinking what they think, seeing what they see. If he doesn't, they are disappointed.
   -- As one to whom everything must be given to make up for their own deprivations. If he isn't grateful, they are disappointed.
   -- As one who will do what they want when they want it.
   -- As one who will be a good parent to them.

> "I could hardly wait for her to grow up."
> "I wanted a companion."
> "I hoped that when she grew up we would always be close, true, friends."

4. But these are wishes which each parent has about the child. Trouble arises when each parent comes up against the other mate's wishes. The child finds himself caught between conflicting demands. Each parent now sees the child as a potential:

   a. Ally against the other mate.
   b. Messenger through whom he can communicate with the other mate.
   c. Pacifier of the other mate.

5. In other words, each parent's wish for an extension of himself gets blocked or challenged by the other parent's wishes.

   a. Individual parenting motivations become confused with the marital conflict.
   b. "Be like me" becomes associated with "Side with me."
   c. Both parents battle for preferred place with the child, mainly because neither feels assured of preferred place with the other. (I have often noted the great concern such parents show as to which parent the baby smiled at first.)

6. The trouble is, the child, by virtue of being either a male or a female, already looks like one parent and unlike the other. He is already sexually identified with one parent.

   a. The mates may at first respond to him as a relatively sexless third member of a triangle, and as a vehicle through whom they can express extension-of-self wishes.
   b. But the child does not remain "sexless" very long, as the parents both respond to the fear of being the left out member of a triangle.
      -- The same-sex parent will see the child as potentially "belonging" more to him.
      -- The other-sex parent will see the child as potentially becoming like the mate and will fear the child's turning against him. So he will work all the harder to woo the child to his side and to try and make up for deficiencies in the marital relationship.

      -- As the other-sex parent tries to use the child as an ersatz mate, the child becomes a pawn in a sex war. So the same-sex parent will also tend to see him as a potential competitor. ("He is _like_ me but _likes_ the other best!")

      -- This is especially true in dysfunctional families because both mates already feel uncertain about their worth in the eyes of the other and, therefore, extra-fearful about being left out.

7. Given this state of affairs, if the child seems to side with one parent, he runs the risk of losing the other parent. Since he needs both parents, making such a choice inevitably hurts him.

   a. The "left out" parent may retreat from and disparage both him and the "chosen" parent, and also fail to fulfill basic parenting functions.
   -- If a boy seems to side with father, mother may say, either overtly or covertly:

   > "What can you expect from males!"
   > "You're just like your father."
   > "What I should have had was a girl."

   -- If a girl seems to side with mother, father may say, either overtly or covertly:

   > "There's women for you!"
   > "You're just like your mother."
   > "What I should have had was a boy."

   -- If a boy seems to side with mother, father may say:

   > "You and your mother are just alke."
   > "Go ahead. Be a mama's boy!"
   > "What red-blooded male likes dolls!"

   -- If a girl seems to side with father, mother may say:

   > "You may be smart, but you're going to find it hard with the boys."
   > "What girl likes mathematics!"
   > "You're your daddy's girl, all right."

   (I should add, however, that when a same-sex parent disparages a child for seeming to ally himself with the other-sex parent, he is not just responding from jealousy. He is also trying to help the child develop behavior which seems most appropriate to his sex. He is, in effect, trying to be a good parent.)

   b. A child is seriously affected when a parent disparages either

him or the other parent <u>or</u> when a parent asks him to side
against the other parent. In the next chapter I will discuss
the development of sex identity, a development which is made
more difficult or is seriously crippled when a parent of either
sex includes the child in the marital relationship.

8. In addition to the problem of who will side with whom in the family triangle, we have found that the mates themselves seem to share the same basic conflicts, even though they may often appear at opposite poles in relation to each other.

   a. Each can project his dislike of attitudes or behavior representing one half of the conflict onto the other parent or onto the child, and fight it there.
   b. Or, together, they can fight half of the conflict by inducing the child to act it out and then punishing him when he does.
   c. Or one parent may take one side of the conflict, the other parent the other side, and in this way attack each other through the child.
   d. This is why one must watch how <u>both</u> parents behave with each other and with the child.

9. The parents find it least threatening to use the child to "cross monitor" the marital conflicts, that is, to be the vehicle through which hostility can be conveyed indirectly to the other partner.

   a. If the parents show hostility toward each other directly, they run the risk of inviting retaliation. (The child cannot retaliate as successfully.)
   b. If the parents try to express their disappointment in each other by scapegoating the environment, they may lose community approval and risk an attack on their self-esteem.

10. If the mates share the same conflicts but are in constant conflict with each other, parental rules about who a child should be and what he should do cannot help but be affected. The rules themselves don't jibe with one another, and they are inconsistently enforced.

    a. An observer of family interaction can come to some fairly reliable conclusions as to what these rules are and how consistent they are, by noting activities which are encouraged, permitted, discouraged, forbidden.
    b. An observer also notes whether both parents explicitly criticize the child's behavior while at the same time they implicitly

encourage it. Both may say, in effect: "Here is your swim
suit. Don't go near the water."

11. The child's behavior as he tries to respond to his parent's unlabeled, contradictory wishes reflects and caricatures the unsolved conflicts existing within and between the mates.

   a. Neither parent, when he uses the child for these ends, is responding to the child as the child is. As Theodore Lidz and
his co-researchers note:

> Indeed... such parents may respond to the child only in
> terms of their own needs displaced to the child, thus build-
> ing up an entire pattern of maladaptive interactions. *

   b. Thus the child is unable to distinguish which of his parents'
reactions are really about him and which are about one or both
of them.

   c. One might also say that by the time a child has lived long
enough in such a learning environment, he does become what
the parents see in him. Parental rules about what he should
do and be become his rules.

12. The process by which parents induce a child to act out their
jointly-held conflicting wishes is, of course, almost entirely
unconscious.

   -- If either parent was aware of how much he influences his
child, he would have to be aware of the child as separate from
himself.

   -- Because of low self-esteem, many parents do not consider
themselves as of enough importance to be a factor in influencing
a child: "He was born that way."

   -- As Jackson puts it:

> All of us are only too eager to deny our effect on our chil-
> dren and others around us -- just as we have little hesita-
> tion in blaming the other guy. It is small wonder that par-
> ents are more intrigued by hereditary and chemical explan-
> ations of their child's emotional problems and it thus be-

---

*T.Lidz, A.Cornelison, S.Fleck and D.Terry. The intrafamilial environment of schizo-
phrenic patients: VI. Transmission of irrationality. *Arch. Neurol. Psychiat.*, 79:
305-316, 1958; p. 311.

comes an unpleasant but necessary part of the psychiatrist's job to assess responsibility without laying blame. *

13. In general, once parents have focused on a child in a dysfunctional way, they may use him much as a dream symbol is used. Yet, as Bell and Vogel point out, the I. P. symbol is different from a dream-symbol:

> While in dreams, any symbolic representation is open to the dreamer, in the family only a very small number of children are available to be used as the potential scapegoats. Hence, when there is a serious... problem, and no child is an appropriate symbol of the problem, there must be considerable cognitive distortion in order to permit the most appropriate one available to be used as a scapegoat. **

14. Once one sees a child being unconsciously used in dysfunctional ways, several questions come to mind:

   a. What if there is more than one child in a family? Which child do the mates unconsciously pick to serve the various I. P. purposes?
   b. Does the same child continue in the I. P. role all his life, or does another child sometimes take over?
   c. Does the sex of the child have anything to do with why one child is assigned the role?
   d. Do families exist in which there is more than one I. P. ?
   e. Each child can be seen as forming the third point in a child-parents triangle. Are children who do not carry out an I. P. function still affected by living in a family which has a dysfunctional child-parents triangle (a triangle which includes in it an I. P.)?

15. We have no research-verified answers as to why marital pairs choose one child as I. P. over another. But from repeated clinical observations we do have some tentative hunches about what leads to the choice. The choice depends, at least in part, on what kinds of conflicts are going on between the mates.

---

*Don D. Jackson. Action for mental illness — what kind? *Stanford Med. Bull.*, 20: 77-80, 1962; p. 78.

**Norman W. Bell and Ezra F. Vogel. The emotionally disturbed child as the family scapegoat. In N. W. Bell and E. F. Vogel (Eds.), *The Family*. Glencoe, Ill: Free Press, 1960; p. 389.

a. Chance characteristics of different children may stimulate
conflicts in the mates.

   -- The child may be ugly, physically deformed, or adopted.
   Such a child increases parental low self-esteem, and also
   stimulates whatever ways the mates have of handling what
   is alien (different-ness). Such a child also threatens the
   parental need to impress the outside environment because
   the child may become the object of neighborhood ridicule
   or curiosity. The parents respond more to protect their
   self-esteem than to protect the child.

   - The child may be especially beautiful or especially intelli-,
   gent. Such a child may increase parental self-esteem while
   at the same time lowering it, as the parents contrast themselves with the child.

   -- The child may look or act like one of his parents or like a
   grandparent, etc. As Bell and Vogel put it:

   > In one family, in particular, this pattern was striking.
   > The father and the eldest child had very similar phy-
   > sical characteristics; not only did they have the same
   > first name but both were called by the same diminutive
   > name by the mother... The wife's concerns about the
   > husband's occupational inadequacy were not dealt with
   > directly, but the focus for her affect was the child and
   > his school performance. *

b. Ordinal position of the child may stimulate conflicts in the
mates.

   -- One parent may have had problems as the middle child in
   his own family, and will now focus on his middle child in a
   special way, fostering sibling rivalry and involving the child
   in the marital relationship. And, as we so repeatedly note,
   when one parent has these problems, the other parent also
   seems to have them.

   -- Or the first child may become the I. P. simply because he
   is available first; he is the first alternative to the mates
   once marital disappointment sets in.

c. Sex of the child may stimulate conflicts in the mates. Parents
may use a child of one sex from birth, or they may use this
child only after he or she has gone through growth changes
which bring out conflicts between the mates.

d. Age of the child may stimulate conflicts in the mates simply
because, as a child grows older, he makes an increasing bid

---

*Bell and Vogel, p. 387.

for independence from parental control. A child may not become the I. P. until he reaches the age of adolescent rebellion. If the mates have conflicts about how much independence is allowable in their own relationship, each adolescent child will receive the dysfunctional parental focus.

e. Simple availability of the child can make him the choice for the I. P. role. One child may be in the home when events put an extra strain on the marital relationship. The child away at school may remain free of the dysfunctional focus.

16. In some families the same child remains the I. P. from birth, but in others the role may be shared or passed on from one child to another.

a. In some families all the female children (or all the male children) will, at one time or another, become I. P. 's.

b. In some families each child becomes an I. P. when he reaches adolescence.

c. In some families two or more children carry on the I. P. function simultaneously. Or they take turns. Or one takes one part of the marital conflict and acts it out; another takes the other part.

17. It is also probable that other children are affected by watching the I. P. family triangle in action, even if they, themselves, were never the subject of dysfunctional parental focus.

a. As I said earlier, if one member of a family has pain which is exhibted in symptoms, all members will, to some degree, react to that pain. They cannot not react.

b. A child learns about people and about himself by interacting with them and by watching them interact. This is why I call any family which has an I. P. in it a dysfunctional family.

18. The next question to ask is: How do the mates unconsciously induce a child to behave in such a way that he eventually gets identified as a "patient"? What does the actual induction process look like and sound like? Here we must take a bypath which leads us into the complex area where communication and symptom development interact.

a. All of us have had the experience of receiving a double-level message from another person who has not made himself clear (see page 83).
-- If a person's words and expression are disparate, if he says one thing and seems to mean another by his voice or his

gestures, he is presenting an <u>incongruent manifestation,</u> and the person to whom he is talking receives a double-level message.

-- I call the whole unsatisfactory interaction a "discrepancy," one which can be easily solved if people are able to be explicit.

-- "What did you really mean?" or, "You don't look as if you really meant that," are common statements about discrepancies, and usually the person who is asked the question is able to be explicit, and the double-level message is clarified. *

b. Thus, by itself, double-level communication need not lead to symptomatic behavior. But under certain conditions, especially where children are involved, it can produce a vice-like situational effect which has been termed the "double bind." (35)

19. What conditions must be present for a child to experience the pressures associated with a double bind?

a. First, the child must be exposed to double-level messages repeatedly and over a long period of time.

b. Second, these must come from persons who have <u>survival significance</u> for him (see pages 45-47).

-- Parents are automatically survival figures because the child literally depends on them for physical life; later, his need for love and approval from them becomes invested with like meaning.

-- In addition, the way the parents structure their messages to the child will determine his techniques for mastering his environment. It is not only his present but his future survival which is in their hands.

-- As a result, he cannot afford to ignore messages from them, no matter how confused.

c. Third, perhaps most important of all, he must be conditioned from an early age not to ask, "Did you mean <u>that</u> or <u>that</u>?" but must accept his parents' conflicting messages in all their impossibility. He must be faced with the hopeless task of translating them into a single way of behaving.

20. Here are a few descriptive examples of the kind of contradictory explicit-implicit messages which help to induce deviant behavior:

---

*The whole subject of incongruent communication, focal for this book, will be treated at length in the chapters on communication theory and will be repeatedly referred to in the analysis of family interaction and therapist intervention in Part Three.

a. A mother tells her daughter to be "a little lady." Yet the first gift she sends her at a girl's detention home is a set of seven, sexy, different-colored brassieres.

b. A father says his son shouldn't defy him. Yet he also complains that his son doesn't stand up to him like a man.

c. A mother and father urge their daughter to stay away from wild parties. Yet they allow her to go to such parties. Then, when she calls her father to ask him to bring her home, mother and father kid her about "being scared" in a provoking, demeaning tone.

21. If the parents' messages to a child are consistently like the ones described above, and if he has acquired no means of challenging them, the child is vitally threatened.

a. He is threatened in his present dependency because he cannot obey on one level of meaning without disobeying on another, and thus continually invites parental rejection.

b. He is threatened as a future adult because he will take his own ways of dealing with the world from the contradictory and self-deceiving pattern to which his parents have accustomed him.

c. Because the conflict within the messages is hidden and the child has oeen trained not to "see" it as the source of his disturbance, he turns the blame on himself (in which he is supported by his parents, who can "see" in this matter no better than he can). He says: "I can never do what is right; I must be bad."

d. On the other hand, on a correspondingly covert level, he is quite aware of the impossible situation in which he has been placed. As a last resort, he may answer covertly himself, using the language of disguised protest which society calls "crazy" or "sick" behavior.

22. However, it may take a long time before the child's behavior becomes so exaggerated that it is recognized by society as deviant.

a. We have already spoken of family homeostasis, a process by which the family balances forces within itself to achieve unity and working order.

b. Ways of acting which would not make sense outside the family, like the behavior of a problem child, may be eminently functional within the family, because it allows the marital partners to keep the focus on the child as troublemaker and divert suspicion from the real troublemaker, which is their own conflicted relationship.

    c. A child's deviant behavior can thus be functional behavior within a dysfunctional family system. (Therefore, if the therapist understands the perceptions and rules by which the marital partners operate, all behavior in the family makes sense.)

23. Since, to the parents, the existence of the "problem child" is profoundly functional, it is not strange if they are unable to evaluate the degree of his disturbance and should try to protect and perpetuate his behavior. But they walk a very thin line. After all, it is this child who holds the power to make or break the magic circle of family balance and he must be treated carefully as a result.

    a. Whichever way he turns, he meets frustration. He can never do what is right because of the contradictory behavior he is asked for, and he can never do what succeeds because he is given such contradictory rules for achieving his goals.

    b. If he becomes too upset, he may produce a symptom so eventful that it can no longer be hidden within the family or incorporated into family functioning.

    c. So he must be covertly rewarded just enough for his disturbing behavior to offset the official disapproval he earns from it, and to offset his frustration in general. As Bell and Vogel state:

> ...in all instances, while the parents explicitly criticized the child and at times even punished him, they supported in some way, usually implicitly, the persistence of the very behavior which they criticized. This permission took various forms: failure to follow through on threats, delayed punishment, indifference to and acceptance of the symptom, unusual interest in the child's symptom, or considerable secondary gratification offered the child because of his symptom.

    d. Here we see the suppleness and maneuverability of double-level rule-giving. Not only does it place the child in the position of being "the bad one," "the failure," but it allows for lifting and lightening of its own pressures when they become too much for the child to bear. And all this can be accomplished covertly, beneath the awareness of either the parent or the child.

24. Thus, the homeostatic system which includes an Identified Patient can remain relatively stable for a long time.

---

*Bell and Vogel, p.390.

a. As we have seen, the parents' expectations create a circular interaction. The I. P. acts out the major conflict within and between the parents. When he thus takes on those characteristics which the parents have induced and fear in themselves and in each other, the child becomes the object of their anxiety and makes their expectations come true.

b. In the following passage, Brodey describes how a child responds to a parent's behavior. Here he is talking about the mother-child relationship, leaving out the influence which an ungratifying marital relationship can have on mothering:

> The infant perhaps would learn that survival within this relationship depended on expressing his own needs in a way and at a time conforming with the mother's projected expectation. The long-term reinforcement of the needs which happened to match the mother's, and the frustration of the needs omitted by the mother, would then alter the child's behavior in the direction of validating the mother's projection. Such a relationship between a mother and her internal image of "her child," now projected onto a real child, who actively conforms with this image, gives a realism to the concept of symbiosis, for the child responded to by the mother is a part of herself. *

25. Eventually, even the environment verifies the I. P. label by officially responding to the I. P. as different, delinquent, or sick. It even siphons off the I. P. for special attention and help, as though the problem does mainly center upon him.

a. Such a labeling and treatment process only helps maintain the system at first, encouraging the parents to rationalize and project even more.

b. They only increase their focus on the I. P., since they now feel inadequate and fear criticism and blame:

> "He had more than I ever did. "
> "He's bad because he wants to be. "
> "The school can't handle him either. "
> "Young people these days are different. "
> "He got in with the wrong gang. "
> "He's no member of this family!"

---

*Brodey, *op. cit.*, p. 385.

c. The community responds with sympathy to the parents, which only corroborates parental belief that the I. P. is, indeed, someone to be concerned about.

26. But as the community experiences more and more of the child's behavior, it begins to examine parental competence. As the finger of blame is pointed at the parents, the family homeostasis begins to break down or become not worth it. The finger of blame moves from the child to the parents as though it were an either-or-proposition.

   a. For one thing, the I. P. victimizes his parents.
      -- He calls on them for extra attention or secondary rewards, with his fits, withdrawal periods, runaways, psychotic episodes, etc. This gives him at least the momentary gratification of being the focus of parental concern.
      -- He requires special consideration as the sick, different, or bad one. As Murray Bowen says:

         The child makes his emotional and verbal demands... by exploiting the helpless, pitiful position. Patients are adept at arousing sympathy and overhelpfulness in others. All the research familes have eventually found their homes geared to the demands of the patient. The. parents are as helpless in taking a stand against the patient as the patient in taking a stand against the parents. *

      -- He manages to get himself exempted from responsibilities,. to be relieved from the necessity of dealing with reality beyond the limits which the family sets for him.
   b. For another thing, his behavior accentuates the husband-wife conflict.
      -- Sons get extra attention from mothers, daughters from fathers. So the basic dynamics of the family triangle become exacerbated.
      --The mates end up blaming each other. As Bell and Vogel put it, the parents privately consider themselves at least partly responsible for the child:

         Thus, the child's disturbance feeds back into the problems which must be faced by the parents, and the mari-

---

*Bowen, *op. cit.*, p. 363.

tal pair often project the responsibility for the child's disturbance onto each other. *

c. Eventually, perhaps, the community takes the I. P. away from the family or recommends/insists on therapy for the family. This challenges the homeostatic balance and also the parents' adequacy as parents. As Haley says (about a psychotic I. P.):

> Although psychotic behavior may serve a function in a family system, a risk is also involved. The patient may need to be separated from the family by hospitalization and so break up the system, or he may enter therapy and change and so leave the system. Typically, the parents seem to welcome hospitalization only if the patient is still accessible to them, and they welcome therapy for the patient up to the point when he begins to change and infringe the rules of the family... **

27. In every respect, a marital relationship which requires an Identified Patient can do nothing but bring disappointment, destructiveness and pain to all three persons.

a. Parental hopes to please and impress the community by having a child who represents the family's ideals can be shattered overnight by I. P. behavior.
b. A parent's hopes that his child will like him can be shattered overnight by I. P. anger and rebellion.
c. Hopes that the child will fulfill a parent's own ambitions can be shattered when an I. P. quits school or gets himself expelled.
d. Hopes that a child will help bring the parents closer together can be shattered when I. P. behavior ends up accentuating marital difficulties.
e. In every way, unsolved marital conflicts boomerang on the mates as they valiantly try to be good parents. And such conflicts cannot help but affect the whole family. As Lidz dramatically describes it:

> ...these marriages... indicate the virtual absence of complementarity.... . Husband and wife do not support each other's needs and the marital interaction increases the emo-

---

*Bell and Vogel, *op. cit.*, p. 397.

**Jay Haley. The family of the schizophrenic: a model system. *J. nerv. men. Dis.*, 129: 357-374, 1959; pp. 373-374.

tional problems of both, deprives the spouses of any sense of fulfillment in life, and deteriorates into a hostile encounter in which both are losers. Instead of any reciprocal give and take, there is demand and defiance leading to schism between partners that divides the entire family, leaving the children torn between conflicting attachments and loyalties. *

28. The Identified Patient, however, suffers the most, in spite of receiving occasional relief from the role, or occasional secondary rewards.

    a. He internalizes the marital conflicts, which makes it difficult for him to maintain gratifying male-female relationships. He continues to live out the family drama with other males and females, and long after the other two participants in the drama are dead.
    b. He feels low self-esteem. His label as the bad, different, or sick one only reinforces his belief in his own worthlessness.
    c. He is inappropriately trained to cope outside the family. As Lidz says about the family of the schizophrenic:

       The world as the child should come to perceive it is denied. Their (parents') conceptualizations of the environment are neither instrumental in affording consistent understanding and mastery of events, feelings, or persons, nor in line with what persons in other families experience. Facts are consistently being altered to suit emotionally determined needs. The acceptance of mutually contradictory experiences requires paralogical thinking. The environment affords training in irrationality. **

29. Here is a brief excerpt from a family therapy session which helps show how conflict between the husband and wife produces symptomatic behavior in the child.

    a. In this excerpt, the induction process is demonstrated indirectly through the conversation of the mates.

---

*T. Lidz, A. Cornelison, S. Fleck, D. Terry. The intrafamilial environment of schizophrenic patients: II. Marital schism and marital skew. *Amer. J. Psychiat.*, 114: 241-248, 1959; p. 246.

**T. Lidz, A. Cornelison, S. Fleck, D. Terry. The intrafamilial environment of schizophrenic patients: VI. Transmission of irrationality. *Arch. Neurol. Psychiat.*, 79: 309-316; p. 311.

b. This marital pair is well on its way to seeing how the marital conflict affects the child.

c. They are also able to discuss the marital relationship as relatively separate from the child. (This contrasts markedly with the inability of parents of a schizophrenic child to discuss their relationship as such.)

d. Once the family therapist can help the mates deal with each other in a more gratifying way, he helps free them to see the child as the child is. Gratifications will then follow for both the child and the parents, since children desperately want to please their parents, and parents basically want to do well by their child.

Excerpt:

W: With the children I have to put them on a double standard too.

Th: Well, why?

W: Well, because my husband can do things, lose his temper and things like that where they're not allowed to. I mean he can pinch and poke them sometimes where they're not allowed to pinch and poke each other when they're irritable.

Th: This obviously introduces a problem which I think...

W: I mean, how can I tell Harry, or sometimes George, not to pinch, not to poke, when my husband does it to Harry?

Th: How do you handle it?

W: Some days I don't. But I prod my husband on these points where he'll, where he would lose his temper, but because I'm prodding him he won't lose his temper and I know that. But still I feel that in not losing his temper that he is getting self-restraint where at one time he would have lost his temper on the same thing without my actually wanting him to really get angry, but still, I...

Th: You want to pay your husband back.

H: That's what she wants to do.

W: I like to see him, uh...

H: That's what she wants to do.

W: I like to see him, I want to see him hold restraint. I like, uh, I don't...

Th: I would think you'd want to pay him back.

H: That's what she does.

W: I do that quite often, too.

Th: Sure, all right, so we look at it. He provokes you; you want to pay him back. You provoke him; he wants to pay you back. I think that's kind of what we've been seeing here, one way or the other, for reasons you haven't understood, but I think this has been going on here. (pause) I don't think you have understood it.

H: See, you're, I mean I feel there's, there's, in other words you're saying that the irritation I've felt about our relationship I've taken out on Harry?

Th: Uh hm. Without meaning to. He's the battleground for both of you.

H: Well you're right and I agree. I've felt this a long time.

30. The induction process, as I have described it, may seem to some readers entirely too one-sided.

   a. What part does the child play in all this? Or are children simply blank sheets upon which their parents write?
   b. Doesn't a child have a choice about accepting or not accepting an I. P. role?
   c. To help answer these questions one must also ask another: What do all children need from their families if they are going to grow up to be functional adults?
   d. In the next chapter we will try to look at the world, not as adults see it, but from a child's point of view.

Chapter VI

What All Children Need in Order to Have Self-Esteem

1. I have been describing marital dysfunction as it affects the parenting of at least one child in a family, the child who becomes an Identified Patient.

   a. If the mates have low self-esteem and little trust in each other, they will expect their child to enhance their self-esteem, to be an extension of themselves, and to serve crucial pain-relieving functions in the marital relationship.
   b. But this sounds entirely too one-sided, as though a child has no choice but to accept the role his parents are asking him to play, or as though children are simply blank sheets upon which their parents write.
      -- Children are not just blank sheets. They come into the world with distinct constitutional differences. (Simply in terms of "body reactivity," newborn infants are markedly different.) They also come into the world as either biological males or biological females.
      -- Yet all children come into the world helpless. Whatever they require for survival must be given to them or taught to them. No child comes into this world with a blueprint of what he shall do and be. This can only come from the people with whom he lives, and whom I call survival figures for this reason.

2. From birth, for example, a child needs to be physically comfortable. He needs to be fed and warm so that the transition from womb to home is as smooth as possible.

3. From birth, a child also needs continuity in relationship.

   a. When food and warmth come, he needs to have the same person bring them, touching him and talking to him.
   b. He needs to have the same human voice and touch introduce him to the existence and predictability of one "other."

    c. Even when he is fed and warm, he learns to require the physical presence of mother; he learns to require relationship per se.

4. A child needs to learn how to influence and predict the responses of others.

    a. As he learns how to differentiate mother from all others, he also learns to develop different mother-influencing responses.
    -- When he cries, food, warmth, and body contact usually come. Yet sometimes they don't come.
    -- Some special kinds of cries work better than others at bringing mother.
    -- Smiles bring extra-special treatment from mother.
    b. When he learns to include father as a survival figure, he will also develop special father-influencing responses.

5. A child needs to learn how to structure the world.

    a. With the help of language, he learns how to differentiate and classify beyond the world of self, father, and mother. He learns to classify cats and dogs, adults and children, males and females, family and not-family.
    b. From his parents he learns not only how to classify but how to evaluate and predict. He learns to differentiate between "good" and "bad" feelings, good and bad behavior, etc.

6. A child needs to esteem himself in two areas: as a masterful person and as a sexual person.* He will develop esteem about himself as a masterful person (a person able to do for himself) if at least one parent validates his developmental growth.

    a. A parent validates this growth when he (or she):
    -- Notes the existence of growth.
    -- Communicates verbally or non-verbally that he notices.
    -- Gives the child increased opportunity to manifest and exercise the new abilities emerging from growth.

---

*I have chosen to separate esteem as a masterful person from esteem as a sexual person for two reasons. First, there are certain abilities and activities which are not necessarily linked with a person's sex. Both males and females learn to work, think, read, problem-solve, experiment. (Of course, because these capacities are shared, they also serve to enrich male-female relationships.) Second, I have noted how some people can have esteem in one area of identity and not in the other. Adults may be able to relate sexually to the other sex but be unable to master themselves or the environment, and vice versa.

b. As the child grows and learns, he becomes increasingly able to do more things for himself, to take care of himself.

-- He can feed himself, go to the toilet by himself, tie his own shoes, anticipate and avoid dangerous objects; in other words, he can handle his own body in relation to the environment and he can manipulate objects.

-- Mastery grows to include the ability to make decisions, to reason, to create, to form and maintain relationships, to time needs in relation to reality, to plan ahead, to tolerate failure and disappointment.

c. To validate a child's mastery, parents must be able to recognize when a developmental stage has been reached and so appropriately time the validation.

-- They must not expect the child to be five when he is eight, or eight when he is five.

-- In other words, for validation to be validation, it must fit the needs, abilities, and readiness of the child. And the acknowledgement of this validation must be clear, direct, and specific.

d. Parental validation does not imply uncritical approval of everything a child wishes to do. Parents are the socializers; they must teach the child that he is not the center of their world or of the world at large.

-- He must learn how to fit in with the requirements of family living, how to balance his needs with those of others, how to fit into the demands of the culture.

-- He needs to develop skills for coping with and balancing the requirements of you, me and the context, at this point in time, under these circumstances.

-- He may scream and complain at restrictions or rules, but accepting restrictions and learning rules is part of growing up. "Restrictions" and "validation" are not opposing terms.

-- Nor does parental validation mean intense, over-solicitous attention to a child's every need. Parents are people, too. Johnny may be ready to walk, with mother's encouragement, but mother, at the moment, may be busy at the stove.

-- Parental validation is most effective when it is administered in a relatively matter-of-fact way.

e. If a parent does not validate a child's ability, or inappropriately times his validation, the child has trouble integrating the ability. It remains a fragmented aspect of the "unimportant me" or the "inadequate me" or the "secret me." Parents may:

-- Fail to see abilities when they are obvious, or give no opportunity for their expression, or show no approval or disapproval when the child manifests them.

-- See abilities prematurely and anxiously urge their expression.

-- See abilities incorrectly (abilities which are simply not there) and anxiously urge their expression.

-- See abilities but discourage and punish their expression.

f. If, when one parent validates a child's abilities, the other parent contradicts the validation, the child's learning will be more difficult and he will manifest what he knows in a more inconsistent way.

-- One parent may expect much from the child, the other parent, little.

-- So a family therapist must be alert to how <u>both</u> parents go about validating each ability in a child.

g. If parents do not validate an ability (if they do not see it, or if they punish it), the child will still continue to grow, since all life is geared toward continuous growth. However:

-- He may not allow himself to manifest the ability.

-- He may manifest it secretly.

-- He may manifest it in a distorted or disguised fashion.

-- In any case, the ability will not contribute to his self-esteem.

7. A child will develop esteem about himself as a sexual person only if both parents validate his sexuality.

a. He must identify with his own sex, yet that very identification must include an acceptance of the other sex.

-- Males validate females as females, females validate males as males.

-- Identification, in this sense, is a two-sided affair: "I am a male in relation to females. It is good to be a male because of what females are."

b. Sexual identification is the result of a three-person learning system. Parents validate a child's sexuality by how they treat him as a small sexual person. But they mainly validate it by serving as models of a functional, gratifying male-female relationship.

-- The context for learning to esteem one's sexuality can be diagrammed like this:

-- A and C are both interactions. B represents the demonstration by husband and wife (as observed by the boy) of adult male-female relations. The demonstration carries the greater weight. (Note that I specify that the child is a little male and his parents are a big male and a big female.)

c. Many people, when they think of families, think of them merely as small groups made up of individuals performing similar or interchangeable role-functions.

-- Family members are not sexless, ageless bodies interacting. They are adult males and females interacting with little males and females.

-- The whole world is made up of males and females. The most psychologically influential roles people play are sex-linked roles. Males are somebody's son, somebody's brother, somebody's boyfriend, somebody's husband, somebody's father, etc. Females are somebody's daughter, etc.

-- Males and females also fill roles which are not sex-linked, such as somebody's boss, somebody's teacher. But usually the sex of that boss or teacher carries special meaning derived from earlier relationships which were sex-linked.

d. If a child needs both sex models, what happens if a boy's father dies when he is born and his mother doesn't remarry? Does this mean that the boy will not develop an esteem about himself as a male person?

-- No, because children are ingenious at creating from the wider environment whatever is missing in family life. They use uncles, grandfathers, older brothers, neighbors, teachers, any available older male.

-- Even children in orphanages make models out of older boys and girls, or out of the housemother and the janitor.

-- Children will also make up a picture of what father was like from all the bits and pieces of data about father which they can receive from mother, grandmother, grandfather, etc.

-- The child will be able to use male models if he receives a message from mother that males are valuable. If he receives a message that males are not valuable and that it hurts mother when he reaches out for models, then he will use available models covertly and in a distorted way.

8. When the parents are not able to validate each other as sexual people, they will not be able to validate the child as a sexual person either.

a. Overt or covert disparagement will be going on between them and they will not provide models of a functional, gratifying, male-female relationship.

b. Moreover, if they are in conflict with each other they will be in conflict with the child, too. He will thus receive contradictory messages from them as to what he should do and be. He will be asked to go north and south at the same time.

c. Also, the parents will use the child as a pawn in the marital conflict. They will ask him to take sides in it. He will often find himself alternately disparaged by one and validated by the other.

d. All in all, he will be subjected to highly contradictory or discrepant experiences.

9. To illustrate, let us break down family interaction into a series of questions which a male child may be said to ask himself. The answers to these questions will form the basis for his sexual identification.

a. How does father (big male) treat mother (big female)?
How does father treat me (little male)?
How does father tell me to treat mother?

How does mother (big female) treat father (big male)?
How does mother treat me (little male)?
How does mother tell me to treat father?

b. I will try to show, under each question, some very simple kinds of contradictions which may be presented to a child.

10. How does mother treat me?
How does father treat me?

a. The child asks himself, in effect: How does mother (or father) react to the fact that I have genitals, that I manifest sexual feelings (in masturbation, nocturnal emissions, erections, etc.), that I manifest sexuality toward others (in sex play, kissing, petting, and later on, in intercourse)? How does mother (or father) react to my interest in toys, my choice of clothes, my fights with boys?

b. This the child can size up for himself because it is a matter of fairly direct experience.
-- He listens to what each says to him. Mother may tell him it is not natural to masturbate. Father may tell him there is no harm in it.
-- He listens to what each says about him to the other. Father may say, "Johnny is a weakling." Mother may say, "He is

not. He is just a boy."
-- He notes how each behaves with him. Father may laugh
when he "plays the field" with the girls. Mother may scold
him for kissing any girl.
-- He notes how each reacts to the other's behavior with him.
Father may spank him when he stays out late. Mother may
then scold father for being too strict.
-- He notes how each tells him to behave and how they themselves behave. Father may tell him not to steal, yet proudly
cheat on his income tax. Mother may tell him not to lie,
yet allow him to pass for twelve instead of fourteen when he
goes to the movies.
c. We must further keep in mind the fact that most children have
the experience of being in the presence of both parents. Thus
the opportunities for inconsistency are multiplied.

11. How do mother and father treat each other?

a. Here the boy does not always have direct experience to go by.
-- How mother and father treat each other includes how they
engage in sexual intercourse. This is usually not observed
by the boy unless he has a chance to do "keyhole" research. *
-- Even if the boy does chance to observe his parents in intercourse, he is not apt to understand the act in its adult meaning; to him it looks as if father is hurting mother. This
would then be data about hurting rather than loving.
b. All that the child can observe directly is how his parents seem
to get along with each other day by day. This, too, may be confusing.
-- He may see them fight during the day, yet sleep in the same
bed at night.
-- He may hear them complain about "apron strings" or "balls-
and-chains," yet see that each one grieves when the other
is away.
-- He may not see them fight openly, yet still observe from
their behavior that they are tense and angry with one another.
-- He may see them looking as though perennially hurt and
not know what the hurt is about

---

*Adults, in our culture, do not openly demonstrate their sexuality before children,
they just give occasional hints about it in jokes, embraces, kisses, etc. I am not
recommending that they demonstrate it, either. But it is interesting to note how
Eskimo children, for example, do not seem to suffer from frequent demonstrations
of their parents' sexuality.

    c. To add to the possible confusion, he must integrate how they treat each other with how they treat him. Consciously or unconsciously he must figure out:

      -- How come mother lets him know when she is hurt or sad, yet never lets on to father?

      -- How come father lets him have anything he wants, yet gripes whenever mother buys a new dress?

      -- How come mother urges him to be the toughest male on the block, yet insists that father keep his temper?

12. <u>How does mother tell me to treat father?</u>
<u>How does father tell me to treat mother?</u>

    a. The child asks: Does mother disparage father, but tell me to treat him with respect? Does father beat up mother, but tell me to treat her with respect?

    b. Many of these contradictory experiences could and would be explained in a functional family because the child could ask about them. The child could then learn that each experience has its own set of variables and is not necessarily linked to a similar one.

    c. In a dysfunctional family, children get the impression that they may not ask questions. Questions might lead to discussions of the marital relationship, and the mates are too pained about that to be able to discuss it openly.

13. When the child is thus left with unexplained contradictions, he will try to explain them to himself, often coming up with incomplete or incorrect conclusions.

    a. In order to come to conclusions, he may dangerously distort or ruthlessly discard the facts of his experience.

    b. For example, he may decide about the male-female relationship that:

      -- If someone is "hurt," the other "inflicts hurt."

      -- If someone is "weak," the other is "strong."

      -- If someone "loses," the other "wins."

      -- If someone is "good," the other is "bad."

    c. Such overly simple black-and-white conclusions make integration of models especially difficult and seriously hamper the development of self-esteem. For example:

      -- The boy can try to reject one parent (which we will call "north") and choose the other parent ("south"). In so doing, he fails to include one sex as a model. Since he <u>cannot</u> unambivalently make such a choice, his rejection of one sex must remain incomplete.

-- He can try to reject both north and south. In so doing, he fails to include either sex as models. He refuses to integrate males in relation to females and females in relation to males, but such a refusal is also incomplete.

-- He can try to integrate what cannot be integrated by trying to go north and south at the same time. In so doing, he remains immobilized in his efforts to use either sex model.

d. A boy's esteem about himself as a male will suffer most if his father looks the most hurt, disparaged, or depreciated in the marital relationship. A girl's esteem will suffer if it is her mother who looks the most hurt.

-- This may be why we so often see sex-linked pathology in families where all the males or all the females manifest pain overtly in symptoms. (Of course, the other children in such families are also feeling pain, even though their pain may not be labeled as pathological.)

-- Since children readily tend to identify with the parent of the same sex (identify in the sense of seeing themselves as genitally like one and unlike the other), it is frightening to see the same-sex parent either inflicting hurt or being hurt.

-- Of the two, however, the thought of being hurt is the more frightening. ("This will happen to me, too!")

-- In spite of other characteristics which stimulate the tendency to see oneself as more like one parent than the other, genital similarity carries with it similar destiny in relation to the other sex.

14. If parents consistently show that they consider their child a masterful, sexual person, and if they also demonstrate a gratifying, functional male-female relationship, the child acquires self-esteem and becomes increasingly independent of his parents.

a. When the time comes for him to partly leave home to attend school, he is confident about doing so (and encouraged to do so by his parents). He is able to profit from substitute parent figures (teachers) for much of his remaining education.

b. Also, as he grows in sexual maturity, he is able to turn away from the family, seek a sexual partner for himself, and set up his own independent life.

c. In choosing a partner, he does not (as Mary and Joe did) seek someone with whom he feels safe or who will bolster his self-esteem. Because he already esteems himself, he is relatively independent of what others think of him (including his mate). So he can take the individuality of his mate into account without

requiring, for his own safety, that the mate be an extension of
him.

d. In every way, self-esteem, independence and individual uniqueness go together.

15. The close relationship between parental validation, self-esteem,
independence, and uniqueness shows up when one observes how
a dysfunctional person (an unvalidated child who is now an adult)
still clings to his parents, or to substitute parent figures, or relates to his sexual partner as if that partner were, in fact, a parent.

a. Such an adult remains in the parental home long after he is
physically grown.

b. Or he continues to be closely involved in his parents' lives. He
moves back in with them later in life. Or he allows them to
move in with him. Or he lives around the corner from them
and sees them so frequently that it is often difficult to distinguish between his home and theirs.

c. Or he leaves his parents but continues to seek validation from
substitute parent-figures outside the home (from an employer,
older friend, etc.). He may label one such figure a "mate" and
marry her, but relate to her as to a parent.

16. Does this mean that when we see parents who have failed to validate their children we can assume they did not want their children to become independent of them? This is partly so, but is
too simple a way to explain the complex motivations involved in
dysfunctional parenting.

a. Parents who fail to validate their children are usually too disappointed in their marital relationship and too involved in fill-
ing their own needs even to see their children as individuals,
much less see their needs. They are themselves products of
dysfunctional parenting.

b. Their failure to validate is more an act of omission than of
commission. They desperately wish to be good parents.

c. Because dysfunctional parents see "parenting" as uninfluenced
by their own pained marital relationship, they are unaware of
the fact that what they build with one hand they tear down with
the other.

Chapter VII

The Family Triangle
A Brief Aside

1. We need to take some time out, before going on to the chapters on communication, to evaluate certain family behavior which seems to contradict the thesis that a child needs his parents to have a functional, gratifying relationship and will automatically thrive if they do have one.

    a. Transcribed excerpts of early family therapy sessions show that:
    -- When husband and wife start to argue, the I. P. intervenes and diverts their focus onto himself.
    -- In the same way, when husband and wife start to get together amicably, the I. P. intervenes and diverts their focus onto himself.
    b. Many psychologists have seen this behavior as emanating from a child's sexual wishes for the other-sex parent. This wish continually leads him to try to separate his parents while at the same time it leads him to bring them together, partly because he fears castration and partly because he needs them both.

2. My own interpretation is somewhat different. To begin with, I do not postulate sex as the basic drive of man. From what I have observed, the sex drive is continually subordinated to and used for the purpose of enhancing self-esteem and defending against threats to self-esteem.

    a. It is true that two people who have high self-esteem, and who openly behave in accordance with their own uniqueness, will come out as sexually identified, masterful, creative people.
    b. However, the need to feel esteem about the self is so important that adult mates will do without sexual satisfaction or fail to demand it in a vital relationship if sexual behavior or demands for it lead to threatened self-esteem. One sees this over and over again when counseling marital pairs.

c. The need for sexual satisfaction continues to exacerbate problems in the marital relationship, but the mates continue in the relationship nonetheless; the need to protect self-esteem, as demonstrated by such marital solutions, takes precedence over the sexual need.

3. I explain the I. P. 's behavior in therapy as follows:

a. When the boy's parents argue, the boy fears that one or both of them may be destroyed in the process.
-- He does not want to lose either parent; he loves and needs them both.
-- He has learned that when he diverts their focus onto himself, his parents stop arguing.

b. When, in family therapy, the boy's parents start to get together amicably, he is presented with an entirely new situation.
-- A boy in a dysfunctional family has never had the experience of united parents. When they tried to appear united, he always knew that they were not. Now, when they might actually be taking their first steps toward amicability, he has no experience by which to evaluate their behavior.
-- Also, up to now his own needs have been met only through their needs. If his parents get together, they may ignore him altogether; he may be abandoned. He has never had the experience of being left out of the marital relationship yet still assured of appropriate parenting.
-- Although his present role as I. P. is a burdensome one, he knows no other family role and, like his parents, he fears change. Both he and his parents actively cooperate to keep family therapy parent-child focused.

c. I have been repeatedly struck by how readily the I. P. drops his role as intervener once family therapy is under way. Once he is assured that arguments do not bring destruction and that marital amicability lightens parental demands on him, the I. P. actively helps the therapist help his parents as mates, while at the same time he tries to get his parents to recognize him as a separate individual with needs of his own. As a matter of fact, the I. P. is often very helpful as "assistant marital counselor. "

4. The question may still be asked, though: Why do we see over-developed father-daughter, mother-son relationships repeatedly showing up in dysfunctional families?

a. Doesn't this prove that each child really is out to separate his parents; that he not only sets out to do so but, in a sense, succeeds? And that when he thinks he has succeeded, he manifests symptoms?

b. Symptoms may, to some degree, originate from the Oedipal conflict. But my question is: How did this conflict come about?

5. I believe that the Oedipal development only becomes an Oedipal "conflict" when the individual is unable to integrate an appropriate picture of his own sex with a compatible picture of the other sex. Whether this happens or not depends on whether the parents are clear, direct and specific in relation to their different-ness and uniqueness.

   a. Children are born with the ability to express feelings about their sexuality toward anyone without guilt.
   b. But children are born into a world which imposes strict taboos on certain expressions and behavior in regard to sexuality. The most important of these is the incest taboo, imposed to protect the child and to protect the adult sexual relationship.
   c. Children learn that the incest taboo exists when they express their feelings toward the other-sex parent and receive disapproval which induces guilt and fear, threatening their self-esteem.

6. But guilt and fear alone do not lead to a crippling Oedipal development.

   a. Children in functional families receive clear, consistent admonishments that neither parent is a suitable object for the child's increasingly strong sexual feelings.
   b. The child of such parents will be "conflicted" by such admonishments to the same degree that he is conflicted by any restraints put on his endless self-wishes.
   c. The child's sexual feelings, per se, are not frowned on. He is assured that such feelings only require expression elsewhere.

7. The incest taboo becomes something to be strongly conflicted about when both parents enforce it inconsistently and one parent positively encourages the child to try and break it.

   a. In dysfunctional families, the other-sex parent fosters incestuous feelings by overtly expressed expectations and demands.
   b. The same-sex parent fosters guilt about such feelings when he fails to intervene with the mate and with the child, yet at the

same time disparages and withdraws from the child, causing the child to drift all the more toward the seductive parent.

c. The incest taboo, by itself, causes only minor conflict in the child. It is the parents' inconsistency about the taboo which both stimulates sexual feelings and increases guilt.

8. As I said before, in any triangle, all three members can have fears about being left out.

a. In my opinion there is no such thing as a relationship between three people. There are only shifting two-person relationships with the third member in the role of observer.

b. In a family triangle, the wife fears that her husband will be less interested in her, the husband fears that his wife will be less interested in him, and the child (when he becomes aware of his father) fears that he will not be the center of his parents' world.

c. By age two a child is definitely aware of his father as a person who is gone all day but who comes home at night, demanding attention from his wife.

-- Children of both sexes respond to the arrival of father with interest and fear. They must now figure out where they fit with two significant others.

-- A child tries to solve the dilemma either by running from one to the other, or by getting both, as a unit, to concentrate on him.

9. In the functional family triangle, the mates are confident about their own marital relationship and so are able, in an unthreatened way, to handle the child's fears of being left out.

a. Mother is able to allow the child a father-child relationship.

b. Father is able to allow the child a mother-child relationship.

c. Yet both mates make it clear to the child that he can never be included in their relationship as mates.

10. In the dysfunctional family triangle, the mates are not confident about their own marital relationship.

a. They already feel left out with each other. (As a matter of fact, one of the principles from which all members in such a family operate is: There is not enough to go around. Who is going to get what is available?) Both mates look to the child to satisfy their unmet needs in the marital relationship.

-- Because they are disappointed in each other and engaged in

a marital war, they both ask the child to side with them.
(This means siding against the other parent.)

-- The mother, in her efforts to turn the boy child into an ally
and ersatz mate, also woos him seductively, offering him
an added inducement. (A father will do the same with his
daughter.)

-- The boy, being a sexual person, will respond to his mother's
affection in kind. He will do so without any feeling of guilt
at first; his mother's behavior will simply look like approval
behavior: "She likes me."

-- The father reacts to the close mother-son relationship with
disapproval, disparagement and withdrawal. The boy receives the message: "Father doesn't like me."

-- And when the boy notes how mother disparages her mate at
the same time that she approves of him, he receives another message: "Mother likes me better than father."

-- The boy loves and needs both of his parents. He can only
feel conflicted by his mother's love: "Mother's love loses
me Father."

b. Incest terrors show themselves, in reality, as learned responses to an actual environment.

-- Mother does show jealousy toward Johnny when Johnny
seems to side with father.

-- Father does show jealousy toward Johnny when mother invites Johnny to become ersatz mate and ally.

-- Yet both parents allow Johnny to think that he is essential
to their marital relationship. When he tries to avoid taking
sides or avoid being used in their sex war, they both continue to involve him.

-- As for Johnny's castration fears, he has good reason to
worry about losing his penis. Since females don't have one,
the penis does come to look like something that could be
taken away by an angry person. (And, more often than not,
he receives just such threats, overtly or covertly, from
either or both parents.)

11. I should add that although a son may appear closer to and allied
with his mother (as a daughter may appear closer to and allied
with her father) such an alliance is illusory.

a. Such a relationship may be interpreted by mother and father
as siding, but it is not siding as far as the boy is concerned.

b. Children cannot unambivalently side with either parent.

c. Children long for and need an accepted relationship with each
parent. This is one of the ways their mastery and sexuality
gets validated.

d. Another way is by example. A mother does not have to engage in sexual intercourse or in seductiveness with her boy in order to assure him of his worth as a male. She indirectly validates him by engaging in intercourse with her husband and by openly enjoying and approving of her husband as a male person. She also validates her son by letting him know that she approves of his sexuality and of his eventually seeking a sexual partner of his own.

12. Because both mates in a dysfunctional family are particularly sensitive about being left out, the child does, in effect, end up by losing one parent unless he is able to reassure both parents by walking the precarious tightrope between them.
   a. The son ends up with a distant relationship to father.
   b. The daughter ends up with a distant relationship to mother.

13. A child who becomes an Identified Patient in a dysfunctional family is saddled with far more than incestuous desires and castration fears.

   a. He is saddled with the burden of believing that he actually does hold his parents together. He learns that he can unite them in some fashion at least by getting them to focus on him.
      -- This happens naturally, as he ricochets from one parent's extension-of-self wishes to the other's.
      -- This also happens as he tries to get validation of himself as an individual with needs of his own and these efforts are perceived as rebellious, unloving behavior.
      -- Since he cannot please both of his parents and also himself, he manifests increasingly contradictory and extravagant behavior.
      -- Such bad, different, crazy or sick behavior leads his parents to unite all the more in an intense focus on him.
   b. But such a way of uniting his parents does not really relieve marital pain, nor does it ever really include the I. P. in the marital relationship. He suffers from a burdensome delusion that he is an "insider." (In a functional family, such a delusion would, as a matter of course, be dispelled.)
      -- The I. P. does not stop his parents' pain. All he does is divert the expression of it onto himself.
      -- He is not a genuine part of the marital relationship. That relationship is a closed system, physically and psychologically. The child is littler than his parents are, he doesn't know what they know, he cannot do what they can do. In no way can he relate to either of them as they can relate to

each other. He is not their equal, sexually or otherwise.

-- Even as an "outsider," the I. P. lacks experience or judgment as to what the pain is all about, so that whatever he does to relieve pain is bound to be unfitting and unsuccessful. (For example, adults may manifest their pain in different ways. Father may show his pain by bullying behavior with mother. Mother may show her pain by crying. To a child, mother thus looks more pained in the marital relationship than father does. How can he fully understand their mutual pain when he sees his parents through such a simple lens?)

c. Even though the I. P. cannot relieve pain, his parents allow him to believe that he can, and that he is essential to the marital relationship. So he suffers from another burdensome delusion: that he is omnipotent.

-- Why would they both respond so intently to him if he were not very important?

-- Why would they both ask him to side with them if he were not equal to them?

-- Why would they both rely on him to validate their self-esteem and represent the family in the community if he were not all-powerful.

-- Why would they rely on him to hold their marital relationship together if he were not a part of it?

-- Who but an omnipotent, omniscient King would be treated in such ways?

d. The I. P. is, in effect, burdened with the responsibility of living for his parents. His own needs are ignored and he has never discovered a way of getting them attended to.

-- As a result, he swings from omnipotence to helplessness, from grandiosity to self-abnegation.

-- He develops little ability to predict in relationships.

-- And, because his needs remain unvalidated, he is distrustful of others, yet dependent to a crippling degree on what others think of him.

PART TWO: COMMUNICATION THEORY

Chapter VIII

Communication: A Process of Giving and Getting Information

1. What do we mean by "communication"? Isn't studying how people communicate almost like studying how they walk across a room? Doesn't this amount to ignoring the deeper processes which psychiatry should deal with?

   a. The word "communicate" is generally understood to refer to nonverbal as well as verbal behavior within a social context. Thus "communication" can mean "interaction" or "transaction." "Communication" also includes all those symbols and clues used by persons in giving and receiving meaning.

   b. Taken in this sense, the communication techniques which people use can be seen as reliable indicators of interpersonal functioning.

   c. As an aid to therapy, a study of communication can help close the gap between inference and observation as well as help document the relationship between patterns of communication and symptomatic behavior. *

2. People must communicate clearly if they are going to get the information which they need from others. Without communication we, as humans, would not be able to survive.

   a. We need to find out about the world. We learn to differentiate and relate ourselves to objects by learning how to label them and by learning, through words and experience, what we can expect from them.

---

*Jackson, Riskin and I demonstrated this several years ago in a paper analyzing five minutes of a taped family conversation which was sent to us without identifying data by Dr. Lyman Wynne. (158)

b. We need to find out about other people and about the nature of relationships.
   -- What, for example, are the socially approved ways to act, ways expected by others?
   -- What behavior will please or displease others?
   -- Why do others respond as they do? What are they after? What are their intentions toward us? What are they reporting about themselves?
   -- How do we appear to others? How do others see us, evaluate us, react to us?
c. We receive this vital information in two basic ways:
   -- We ask for verbal responses.
   -- We also observe nonverbal behavior.

3. People must communicate clearly if they are going to be able to give information to others. We need to let others know what is going on inside us.

   a. What we have learned or what we think we know.
   b. What we expect of others.
   c. How we interpret what others do.
   d. What behavior pleases us, displeases us.
   e. What our own intentions are.
   f. How others appear to us.

4. Let us examine in this chapter the difficulties posed by simple verbal communication.

   a. For one thing, the same word can have different meanings, different denotations.
      -- For example, if B asks us "What class are you in?" it is not clear whether he is asking us what we are taking in school or what social standing we have.
      -- In the United States, "Let's table that motion" means "Let's put it aside." In England, the same phrase means "Let's bring it up for discussion."
   b. For another thing, the same word can have different connotations.
      -- For example, "mother" is a woman who bears and/or rears a child (denotation). But "mother" can be a warm, accepting, nurturing woman or a cold, demanding, unresponsive woman (connotation).
      -- When B uses the word "mother," what connotation does the word carry for him?
   c. What compounds the problem is that words are abstractions,

symbols which only stand for referents.

-- The symbol is not the same as the "thing" or "idea" or "observation" for which it stands (although we often behave verbally as if symbols are literally what they symbolize). Very often the symbol and its meaning are assumed to be synonymous.

-- Also, words are at different levels of abstraction. We have words about objects, words about relationships between objects, words about inner states, words about other words, words about words about words.

-- As words become more abstract, their meanings can become increasingly obscure.

-- Finally, there are many aspects of experience which are not describable by words.

5. This elementary "meaning of words" aspect of communication is very important because people so often get into tangles with each other simply because A was using a word in one way, and B received the word as if it meant something entirely different.

   a. An excellent example of this might be when A says, "I was only a little late," and B says, "You were not!"

   b. Because words themselves are often unclear, it is important for people to clarify and qualify what they say, and to ask others to do the same when they find themselves puzzled or confused.

6. Words are tools which people use to give and get information. If a person fails to realize that words are only abstractions he will tend to overgeneralize, and he will fall into the error of making the following assumptions:*

   a. He will assume that one instance is an example of all instances. He will be unclear, particularly in his use of who, what, where, and when.

      -- He may use the concept who as follows:

         "Everybody is like that."
         "Nobody likes me."
         "All women are..."
         "Men are..."

*I am indebted here to William Pemberton's article, "Non-Directive Reorientation in Counseling." (200)

-- He may use the concept <u>what</u> as follows:

> "<u>Nothing</u> turns out right."
> "<u>Everything</u> is all fouled up."

-- He may use the concept <u>where</u> as follows:

> "<u>Everywhere I</u> go, that happens."
> "<u>Nowhere</u> is it any different."

-- He may use the concept <u>when</u> as follows:

> "<u>Never</u> is it any different."
> "<u>Always</u> this happens to me."

b. He will assume that other people share his feelings, thoughts, perceptions:

> "How can you like fish!"
> "Why didn't you do it the <u>right</u> way?"
> "Of course he wouldn't want that!"

c. He will assume that his perceptions or evaluations are complete:

> "Yes, I already know about that."

d. He will assume that what he perceives or evaluates won't change:

> "That's the way she is."
> "I've always been that way."
> "That's life."

e. He assumes that there are only two possible alternatives when assessing perceptions or evaluations; he dichotomizes or thinks in terms of black or white:

> "She either loves me or she doesn't."
> "That will either make him or break him."
> "You're either for me or against me."

f. He assumes that characteristics which he attributes to things or people are part of those things or people:

"That picture is ugly."
"He is selfish."
"She is hostile."

g. He assumes that he can get inside the skin of another. He operates as if from a "crystal ball" and he acts as a spokesman
for others:

"I know what you're thinking."
"I know what she really means."
"I will tell you what she was feeling."
"This is what he was going through."

h. He also assumes that the other can get inside his skin. He
assumes that the other also has a crystal ball. He allows the
other to be a spokesman for him:

"She knows what I think."
"You know what I really mean."
"He can tell you what I went through."

7. If the receiver of these messages is as dysfunctional a communicator as the sender, he will respond by either agreeing or disagreeing.

a. If he agrees, clear communication will not have taken place,
since he cannot be sure what it is to which he is agreeing.
He may say:

"That picture is ugly, isn't it."
"She is selfish, isn't she."
"Yes, she was feeling such and such."
"Yes, women are like that."
"That certainly is the right way."

b. If he disagrees, he still cannot be sure with what he is disagreeing. However, the fact that he does disagree can stimulate either him or the sender to clarify their messages later.
He may say:

"That picture is not ugly. It is beautiful."
"She is not selfish. She is very generous."
"No, she was not feeling that. What she was feeling was..."
"No, women aren't like that. They're..."
"No, that isn't the right way. This is the right way."

8. If the receiver, in this interchange, is a functional communicator, he will not stop either to agree or disagree. He will first ask the sender to clarify and qualify. He may say:

> "What do you mean when you say that picture is ugly?"
> "What does she do that strikes you as selfish?"
> "How can you tell what I'm thinking? You aren't me."
> "What do you mean,'everybody'is like that? Do you mean your wife, your boss, or who?"
> "Do you mean all women or just the women you have known?"
> "What doesn't turn out right? What in particular?"
> "Where, exactly, have such things happened to you? At home? At work?"
> "Why does it surprise you that I like fish? You don't, but that doesn't mean I don't."
> "What do you mean by doing something the 'right' way? Do you mean your way, or what?"

9. Once the sender receives such requests to clarify and qualify, how does he respond to them?

a. If he is a functional communicator, he may say:

> "Let me try to re-state that another way."
> "Maybe I should give some examples."
> "I operate from a certain assumption on this, I guess. Here's what I must be assuming..."
> "I overgeneralized, didn't I? I'll try to pin that down a bit more."
> "I'm giving my impression. Maybe you don't share it. How do you see it?"

b. If the original sender is a dysfunctional communicator, he can respond to requests to clarify or qualify in a multitude of different ways. But all these ways tend to shut out feedback from the other.

-- He may openly rebuff such requests:

> "You know perfectly well what I mean."
> "I couldn't be any clearer."
> "You heard me."

-- He may restate his case without altering it:

> "As I said, women are..."

-- He may re-emphasize his case, without altering it:

> "Women are not only X, they are also Y."
> "That picture is not only ugly, it is positively revolting."

-- He may accuse the questioner:

> "Why get so 'picky'?"
> "You don't understand plain language."
> "Must you 'peel and shred'?"

-- He may evade the questions. (See pages 86-88 for an elaboration of this communication technique.)

10. If the original sender responds in a functional way to requests for clarification and qualification, then the receiver of his message has a better idea of what is being discussed. He may then say:

> "Oh, that's what you meant! I misunderstood you."
> "Well, we have different ideas about that. Let's see how we arrived at them."
> "I don't share your experiences, I guess."
> "Yes, I've had similar experiences, but I came to slightly different conclusions. Here's what I decided..."
> "Maybe we are hung up on words. Here's what I mean by..."

11. If the sender had clarified and qualified his messages in the first place, the interchange would have had less chance of going awry. He might have said:

> "Many people, at least the ones I have known, seem like that."
> "This often happens to me, particularly at work."
> "I find it hard to see how anyone could like fish. Maybe that's because I hate it."
> "This way has worked for me. Maybe it would for you."
> "I wouldn't expect him to want that. I wouldn't want it myself."
> "I would call her selfish, but then she is probably different with other people. How is she with you?"
> "To me, women are such and such. Do you agree?"
> "I got the impression, from what you said, that you meant to do such and such. Did I size you up right?"

12. In summary, a person who communicates in a functional way can:

   a. Firmly state his case,
   b. yet at the same time clarify and qualify what he says,
   c. as well as ask for feedback,
   d. and be receptive to feedback when he gets it.

13. If verbal communication is to be reasonably clear, both the sender of a message and the receiver have the responsibility to make it so.

   a. Mutual clarification and qualification cuts down on generalizations.
     -- It enables both parties to be specific and to give evidence for their assertions.
     -- It enables one person to check out his "reality" against the other person's "reality."
   b. It also helps to separate the perceiver from what is being perceived.
     -- It cuts down on the tendency to project one's own wishes, thoughts, perceptions, onto others.
     -- It cuts down on the efforts of one person to speak for another.

14. Of course, none of us communicate this ideally or intellectually.

   a. We all generalize when we communicate.
   b. Anyone who perpetually clarified and qualified would seem just as dysfunctional as the person who rarely did so. He might even lead the receiver to wonder if there was anyone in the interaction to interact with.
   c. A sender who perpetually asked a receiver for feedback would put himself in the position of being inundated by it and never formulating his own case.
   d. A receiver who perpetually asked a sender to clarify would seem testy, uncooperative, and irritating.

15. Generalizations are dangerous, if overused, but they are also indispensable shortcuts.

   a. They help us organize our experience.
   b. They help us talk about a multitude of different observations all at once.
   c. They free us from the necessity of evaluating every new event afresh.

d. Theory itself is a body of generalizations. As such it has been a useful tool in all the sciences.

16. But the person who communicates dysfunctionally behaves as though he is not aware of the fact that he generalizes or that he operates from assumptions.

    a. He rarely checks out or specifies how he or others are using words.
    b. He overgeneralizes.
    c. His communication techniques only serve to becloud meaning, and he seems to have no way to get back on the communication track when he gets off of it.

17. Dysfunctional people also send incomplete messages.

    a. They do not complete their sentences, but rely on the receiver to fill in:

> "He isn't very... you know. "
> "As you can see... well, it's obvious. "

    b. They use pronouns vaguely. (Such communication problems repeatedly show up in family therapy.)

> W: We went and so they got upset.
>
> Th: Wait a minute. Who went where? Who got upset?
>
> W: Oh, well, Harry and I went to his mother's house, see -- Harry's mother's house. The kids wanted to go but Harry and I wanted to go alone. So the kids cried as we left the house.

    c. They leave out whole connections in their messages.

> Th: (to wife) I'm sorry I was late to our appointment today.
>
> W: Oh that's all right. Mark was running around the block.

Filled in, such a message becomes:

> Oh that's all right. My dog got out of the house (my dog's name is Mark) and was running around the block. I had to run after him. It took some time to catch him. So I was late to our appointment, too.

    d. Often, they do not send a message at all but behave, in relation to others, as if they had. (This comes up repeatedly in therapy, and is usually related to an inside wish which never gets into words.)

M: They never help around the house.

Th: Now you mean the kids?

M: Yes.

Th: Have you told them what you want them to do?

M: Well, I think so. They're supposed to know.

Th: But have you <u>told</u> them?

M: Well, no.

* * * * * * *

W: We had no bread for dinner. He forgot.

Th: You mean your husband?

W: Yes.

Th: (to husband) Did you know that you were out of bread in the house?

H: No, heck no, I didn't. . . .

Th: Do you remember her telling you?

H: No. No, she never told me. If I had known, I would have picked some up on the way home.

Th: Do you remember telling him that you were out of bread and asking him to pick some up?

W: Well, maybe I didn't. No, maybe I didn't. But you'd think he'd know.

e. Here is an example which also includes a tangle over the definition of a word:

H: She never comes up to me and kisses me. I am always the one to make the overtures.

Th: Is this the way you see yourself behaving with your husband?

W: Yes, I would say he is the demonstrative one. I didn't

know he wanted me to make the overtures.

Th: Have you told your wife that you would like this from her -- more open demonstration of affection?

H: Well, no, you'd think she'd know.

W: No, how would I know? You always said you didn't like aggressive women.

H: I don't, I don't like <u>dominating</u> women.

W: Well, I thought you meant women who make the overtures. How am I to know what you want?

Th: You'd have a better idea if he had been able to <u>tell</u> you.

18. As I said before, absolutely clear communication is impossible to achieve because communication is, by its very nature, incomplete. But there are degrees of incompleteness. The dysfunctional communicator leaves the receiver groping and guessing about what he has inside his head or heart.

   a. He not only leaves the receiver groping and guessing; he operates from the assumption that he did, in fact, communicate.
   b. The receiver, in turn, operates from what he guesses.
   c. It is easy for them to misunderstand one another.
   d. It is difficult for them to arrive at planned goals or outcomes.
   e. People need to have a means for completing their communication as much as possible if they are going to arrive at successful joint outcomes, from accomplishing the mundane work of everyday life and seeing that the bread gets on the table, to being able to enjoy mutually satisfying sexual relationships.

19. This is not to say that all incomplete messages are dysfunctional ones. They may be functional and amusing.

   a. Codes, for instance, are intentionally incomplete messages.
     -- They represent shared shortcuts in meaning.
     -- People who share a code share something special together.
   b. But the users of a code must be clear about its meaning. When they get off the communication track through using codes, they must be able to get back on the track by being able to determine when the game is over.
   c. When people have shared experiences, they tend to condense many of them into codes. Therapists do this with patients. "Oh, that's all right, Mark was running around the block,"

became a code between the family and me, a code which I referred to when family members failed to complete their messages. I also used it to demonstrate that codes <u>can</u> be used functionally, if everyone concerned is clear about the meaning. This code got shortened to "Remember Mark" or even just "Mark."

d. There is a story about codes, which I often tell to patients when they get off the communication track with each other:

> A reporter visited an old men's home and noticed a group of men sitting in the living room. One of the men said "27" and everyone went "ha ha ha." Then another said "15" and everyone went "ha ha ha." Then another said "36" and there was silence.

> "What's going on here?" the reporter asked the director, who was showing him around. "You hear all these numbers and then everyone laughs."

> "Oh," the director said, "you see, these men have been here for a long time and they know each other's jokes so well that instead of telling them over and over again, they just give the number."

> "Well," the reporter asked, "what happened to number '36' then?"

> "Oh that fellow!" the director answered, "He never <u>could</u> tell a joke."

Chapter IX

Communication: A Verbal and Nonverbal Process
of Making Requests of the Receiver

1. When judging whether a communication is clear, one must also remember that people communicate in a variety of ways in addition to using words.

   a. A person simultaneously communicates by his gestures, facial expression, body posture and movement, tone of voice, and even by the way he is dressed.
   b. And all this communication occurs within a context. When does it take place? Where? With whom? Under what circumstances? What is the contract between the persons carrying on the interchange?

2. Because of all these factors, communication is a complex business. The receiver must assess all the different ways in which the sender is sending messages, as well as being aware of his own receiving system, that is, his own interpretation system.

   a. When A talks, B assesses the verbal meaning of A's message.
   b. He also listens to the tone of voice in which A speaks.
   c. He also watches what A does; he notes the "body language" and facial expressions which accompany A's message.
   d. He also assesses what A is saying within a social context. The context may be how B has seen A respond to him and to others in the past. It may also be B's expectations about what the requirements of the situation are.
   e. In other words, the receiver (B) is busy assessing both the verbal and the nonverbal content of A's message so that he can come to some judgment about what A meant by his communication.

3. What A meant by his communication can be said to have at least two levels:

    a. The denotative level: the literal content.

    b. The metacommunicative level: a comment on the literal content as well as on the nature of the relationship between the persons involved.

4. Animals other than man can send metacommunications. For example, as Gregory Bateson describes it:

    a. Cats may go through all their battery of fighting motions yet at the same time withhold their claws.

    b. By this metacommunication the cat clues other cats as well as people to the fact that he is not "really" fighting; he is playing at fighting. (20)

5. Metacommunication is a message about a message.

    a. It conveys the sender's attitude toward the message he just sent: "The message I sent was a friendly one."

    b. It conveys the sender's attitude toward himself: "I am a friendly person."

    c. It conveys the sender's attitude, feelings, intentions toward the receiver: "I see you as someone to be friendly with."

6. Humans are especially versatile at metacommunication.

    a. Humans, like other animals, can send nonverbal metacommunications. But the variety of these is wide; humans can frown, grimace, smile, stiffen, slump. And the context in which humans communicate is, itself, one way of communicating.

    b. As a matter of fact, humans cannot communicate without, at the same time, metacommunicating. Humans cannot not metacommunicate.

    c. Humans can also send verbal metacommunications. They can verbally explain their message-sending.

7. When a person verbally explains his message-sending, he is thus denotatively speaking at a metacommunicative level. And these verbal metacommunications are, themselves, at various abstraction levels.

    a. A person can label what kind of message he sent telling the receiver how seriously he wishes him to receive it and how he should respond to it. He can say:

"It was a joke." (laugh at it)
"It was just a passing remark" (ignore it)
"It was a question." (answer it)
"It was a request." (consider it)
"It was an order." (obey it)

b. He can say why he sent the message, by referring to what the other did.

"You hit me. So I hit you back."
"You were kind to me. I was returning the favor."

c. He can say why he sent the message, by referring to what he thinks the other's wishes, feelings, intentions toward him are.

"I thought you were mad and were going to hurt me."
"I thought you were tired and wanted me to help you."
"I thought you were discouraged and wanted me to reassure you."

d. He can say why he sent the message by referring to a request made by the other:

"You were ordering me to do something, and I don't take orders."
"You were requesting something from me, and I was considering it."

e. He can say why he sent the message by referring to the kind of response which he was trying to elicit from the other:

"I was trying to get your goat."
"I was trying to get you to love me."
"I was trying to get you to talk."
"I was trying to make you laugh."
"I was trying to get you to agree with me."

f. He can say why he sent the message by specifically referring to what he was trying to get the other to do or say or not do and not say: ,

"I wanted you to go to the store for me."
"I was asking you to phone her for me."
"I was asking you to leave the room."
"I didn't want you to tell her about my illness."
"I wanted you to tell him that I was home."

8. Since humans can "metacommunicate" both verbally and nonverbally, they can give the receiver quite an assortment of messages to sort and weigh, as he tries to figure out what is meant
   by the communication.

   a. Perhaps A makes the following denotative statement: "The
   dog is on the couch."

   b. He automatically comments, nonverbally, on this statement,
   by the irritable tone in which he makes it.

   c. He can then verbally explain what he meant by what he said.
   Out of the welter of choices, he may say: "I wanted you to
   take the dog off the couch."

9. The receiver of these messages (B) must balance what A said,
   with how he said it, with what he then said about it.

   a. B balances the nonverbal and the verbal metacommunications
   (within the context) and compares them to the denotative statement.

   b. If they are all congruent (seem to jibe with each other) he has
   little difficulty in deciding that A meant what he said he meant.

   c. Whether or not they jibe, he will attend more to the nonverbal
   metacommunications and to context than he will to the verbal
   metacommunications. For one thing, the nonverbal is a less
   clear or explicit communication, so it requires greater attention.

10. Whenever a person communicates he is not only making a state-
    ment, he is also asking something of the receiver and trying to
    influence the receiver to give him what he wants. This is the
    "command aspect" of a message. Such requests, however, may
    have various degrees of explicitness and intensity.

   a. The sender may be simply asking the receiver to show, by
   response, that his message was heard: "Just listen to me."

   b. Or he may be asking for a specific kind of response: "Tell me
   where the store is" or, "Go to the store for me."

11. The receiver, in turn, must respond, because people cannot <u>not</u>
    communicate.

   a. Even if the receiver remains silent, he is still communicating.

   b. And, incidentally, symptoms are one way of communicating in
   a nonverbal way.

12. But even though all messages have requests in them, they are not always expressed verbally. Thus, the receiver must rely on metacommunications for his clues as to what the sender wants. He asks himself:

   a. What is the sender verbally saying?
   b. What, specifically, is he requesting? Is the request fully expressed at the denotative level?
   c. If not, perhaps the way in which he communicates and the context in which he is communicating will give me clues to what he is asking of me.

13. If the communication, or message, and the metacommunication or meta-message do not fit, the receiver must somehow translate this into a single message. In order to do this satisfactorily he needs to be able to comment on the presence of the discrepancy. Let us take a trivial example. A husband who is working on a household fixture says, in an irritable tone, "Damn it, the fixture broke!" The wife, in this relationship, may go through the following process (with greater agility and speed, of course, than the snail's pace described here):

   a. He is telling me about the condition of the electrical fixture he is working on.
   b. But he is doing more than that. He is telling me that he is irritated. His "Damn it," along with his tone, helps me decide this.
   c. Is he criticizing me? Is he telling me that I am responsible for the condition of the fixture?
   d. If he is criticizing me, what does he want me to do? Take over the job for him? Apologize? Or what?
   e. Or is he criticizing himself, irritated that he is having a frustrating time with the job, and that he only has himself to blame for the fact that the fixture broke?
   f. If he is primarily criticizing himself, what is he asking me to do? Sympathize with him? Listen to him? Or what?
   g. I know, from living with him, that he prides himself on his tool dexterity and that he considers electrical maintenance his special forte. Evidently, his view of himself is being put to the test. So he must be criticizing himself. And he must primarily be asking me to sympathize with him.
   h. But sympathize how? Does he want me to help him with the job, bring him coffee, or what? What behavior on my part that he could see and hear would mean to him that I am sympathizing with him?

14. Let us take another example. A husband says, in an irritable tone, "The dog is on the couch." The wife, in this relationship, may go through the following process:

    a. He is telling me where the dog is.
    b. But he is doing more than that. He sounds irritated.
    c. Why is he telling me about his irritation? Is he criticizing me for the fact that the dog is on the couch?
    d. If he is not criticizing me, what does he want me to do? Just listen to him? Sympathize with his irritation? Take the dog off the couch? Or what?
    e. I wanted a dog. He didn't. I went ahead and got one without his agreement. Now, when he shows his irritation at the dog, he is complaining about what I did. He is criticizing me for disobeying him. He undoubtedly wants me to take the dog off the couch, but does he also want me to get rid of the dog and apologize to him for going against his wishes?

15. Let us return to the first example. Instead of saying, "Damn it, the fixture broke", the husband could say, "Damn it, I'm having a hard time with this job. Bring me a cup of coffee." The wife, in this case, would have little trouble assessing his message. He would be telling her overtly what he wanted from her and why. In other words, his request that she sympathize with him by bringing coffee would be clear.

16. In the second example, instead of saying, "The dog is on the couch," the husband could say, "Take the dog off the couch and get rid of him. You never should have bought a dog. I told you I didn't want one." The wife in this case would have little trouble assessing his message.

    a. He would be telling her specifically what he wanted from her and why. In other words, his request that she agree to obey him would be clear.
    b. In both cases, the wife is still in the position of deciding whether or not to agree to her husband's request that she obey him. But at least she is in no doubt about what it really is that her husband wants of her.

17. In other words, the request, which is part of every message, may or may not be expressed denotatively. And there are degrees to which requests can be spelled out denotatively.

    a. "Damn it, the fixture broke," and "The dog is on the couch," are very indirect requests, requests not expressed at the denotative level.

  b. "Bring me a cup of coffee," and "Take the dog off the couch and get rid of him," are direct requests, requests expressed at the denotative level.
  c. Or, if these specific requests had been expressed at a more abstract level, they would also be direct: "Sympathize with me" or "Do what I want."

18. However, all messages, when viewed at their highest abstraction level can be characterized as "Validate me" messages. These are frequently interpreted as "Agree with me," "Be on my side," "Validate me by sympathizing with me," or, "Validate me by showing me you value me and my ideas."

19. When people communicate, they rarely go around verbally requesting that others agree with them or requesting that others want what they want. They don't, because they are forced by the wish to be valued, and by the wish for cooperation, to persuade or at least try to elicit the wished-for response. Many persons feel embarrassed about their wish to get validation from outside themselves.

  a. As I have said, communication is a necessarily incomplete process. But we can now see why this process becomes even more incomplete than pure logic or inadequacy of words would dictate.
  b. Incomplete (indirect) communication can serve many interpersonal purposes which are not necessarily dysfunctional.
     -- It can help camouflage such requests.
     -- It can prevent embarrassment in case one's requests (of any kind) are refused.

20. Up to now, I have been discussing the problems posed for human receivers by the complexity and the incompleteness of human communication.

  a. Just because this communication is complex and incomplete to differing degrees, all receivers are required to fill in or complete the sender's message by clairvoyance or guesswork.
  b. Receivers can and do achieve this, sometimes with amazing accuracy, considering all the fancy footwork they have to go through.
  c. But there are times when even the most clairvoyant of receivers guesses incorrectly. When this happens, the sender's next message usually lets him know his error.

21. The messages I have listed in this chapter have all been relatively congruent within the context; they have jibed with each other.

   a. A congruent communication is one where two or more messages are sent via different levels but none of these messages seriously contradicts any other. For example, the husband says, "The dog is on the couch," in an irritable tone, in a context which tells the wife that he is irritated and why he is irritated.

   b. An incongruent communication is one where two or more messages, sent via different levels, seriously do contradict each other. One level of communication is context itself. For example, the husband says, in a delighted tone, that the dog is on the couch, but from the context the wife knows that he hates dogs; whether they are on couches or anywhere else.

22. Simple contradictory communication is where two or more messages are sent in a sequence via the same communication level and oppose each other.

   a. Perhaps A says the following:

        "Come here... No, go away."
        "I love you... No, I hate you."
        "I'm happy... No, I'm sad."
        "My wife is tall... No, my wife is short."

   b. Perhaps A does the following:
    -- Pushes B away. Pulls B back.
    -- Buys a ticket to the movie, but doesn't go see it.
    -- Puts his coat on, then takes it off.

23. But such simple contradictions cannot occur without some accompanying metacommunication, since one cannot not metacommunicate.

   a. Although the self-contradictions listed above are relatively clear, they are also accompanied by smiles or frowns or tone of voice, and in a context.

   b. When contradictions occur between different levels of communication, they become incongruent. *

---

*"Incongruent" refers to a discrepancy between the report and the command aspects of a message; for the system for analyzing this devised by Bateson, Jackson, Haley and Weakland, see 35, 114, 146, 158, in the bibliography.

24. Messages differ in the degree to which they are incongruent. Relatively simple incongruent communication sounds and looks like this:

   a. A says, "It's cold in here," and takes off his coat.
   b. A says, "I hate you," and smiles.
   c. A wears an evening dress to a funeral.
   d. A wears tennis shoes to a board of directors' meeting.
   e. A says, "Come closer, darling," and then stiffens.

25. Incongruent communication can become even more so when the sender's nonverbal metacommunication does not jibe with his verbal metacommunication.

   a. The sender may say "Come closer, darling," then stiffen, and then say, "I want to make love."
      -- In this case, should the receiver respond to the sender's denotative statement ("Come closer, darling.")?
      -- Or should he respond to the sender's nonverbal statement (the stiffness)?
      -- Or should he respond to the sender's words explaining his intentions ("I want to make love.")?
      -- This is called being presented with a double-level message.
   b. As usual, the receiver relies heavily on context, and on the nonverbal signals to help him in his clairvoyance process. In this case, the nonverbal signals and the context contradict each other. But, being an especially trusting and courageous receiver, he says to himself:

      "Let's see. The sender and I are courting. Yet other people are around.

      "I have learned from past experience with the sender that she is nervous about showing amorous feelings publicly. But that doesn't mean she doesn't have amorous feelings toward me.

      "I will live dangerously and ignore her nonverbal metacommunication in this case. I will rely on context alone and accept her verbally-stated intention.

      "In other words, her verbal statement 'I want to make love' carries greater weight with me. All I do is add to it the proviso which she did not add: '...but other people are around, so I am just nervous.' In other words, the sender is willing to be nervous, with a little assistance."

c. The freedom to comment and question immediately takes the receiver out of the clairvoyant dilemma. When this freedom is not present, the chances for misunderstanding are great. In the case of a child, as we have seen, there is a likelihood that such messages will be built up to the point where a "double bind" occurs (see page 36).

26. Incongruent communication like that just described puts an extra burden on the receiver. But, whether or not the sender's message is incongruent, the receiver can still go through various checking-out procedures in order to find out what is being reported, what requested, and why.

a. For example, when the wife heard her husband say, in an irritable tone, "Damn it, the fixture broke," she could have decided that she still didn't have enough data, even from the content of the message, to find out what her husband was requesting from her and why.
b. She might have gone to where he was and stood there for a minute, continuing to pick up clues from him.
   -- If she had done this, she would, of course, have been communicating with him. By her presence she would be saying: "I heard you. I am attending."
   -- He would also continue to communicate with her, as he jabbed at the fixture, grunted, sighed, etc.
c. The wife might then have asked, "Is there anything I can do?"
   -- The minute she did this, she would be asking her husband to be specific in what he was requesting.
   -- Perhaps he would have said, "No, I just have to work it out."
   -- By this response, the wife would have succeeded in narrowing her unknowns. She would now be more certain that he was distressed with himself but she still could not be sure what he specifically wanted from her. Did he want her to listen? Attend? Sympathize?
d. The wife might go on to ask, "Would you like a cup of coffee?" And he might answer, "Yes, damn it, I would." The communication sequence would now be relatively closed or complete. (Of course, it is more complete if she actually brings the coffee!")

27. If, instead, the wife had been fairly confident about her clairvoyance, she might have simply assumed that she knew what his im-

plied request was. She might have put it in words herself and seen how he responded.

a. She could have asked outright, "Would you like a cup of coffee?" and he might have said, "Yes, damn it, I would." If she had guessed correctly enough, the sequence would have been relatively closed.

b. But he might have said, "Hell, no, what would I want coffee for, at a time like this?" Then she would have known that her clairvoyance process wasn't working very well. She would have been required to check out further, perhaps by going through the clue-getting procedures already described.

28. Receivers vary in their ability to perceive the needs and wishes of others.

a. Although all receivers put great weight on the metacommunicative aspects, they vary in their ability to assess what the sender is asking of them.

-- The wife may mistake her husband's irritation with himself for a criticism of her, and end up trying to take over the job for him instead of sympathizing with him.

-- The wife may mistake her husband's criticism of her for irritation over the specific behavior of the dog, and end up trying to sympathize with him instead of taking the dog off the couch or getting rid of the dog.

-- The lover, in the third example, may mistake the woman's stiffening for distaste, and end up rejecting her instead of making love.

b. We even have psychiatric labels for people who are not able to accurately weigh a message for its meaning. They are not able to guess attitudes, intentions, feelings (as expressed in metacommunication) accurately.

c. If this wife, in all contexts, in all relationships, and at all times within a relationship, decides that senders are criticizing her or praising her, we would readily label her paranoid or egocentric.

d. Also, although receivers put great weight on the metacommunicative aspects to help tell them what the sender is requesting, they vary in their ability to attend to denotation in spite of, or along with, metacommunication. For example, perhaps a person attends a lecture for the purpose of receiving denotative content from the speaker. But perhaps the speaker speaks in such a frightened tone that the receiver cannot hear what the speaker is saying because he is so concerned about the speaker's fright.

29. Senders vary in their ability to send clear requests, so that the receiver has to guess as little as possible.

   a. For example, let us say that a wife wants to see a movie with her husband. If she communicates in a functional way, she might say, "Let's see a movie," or, more overtly, "I would like to see a movie with you."

   b. But, if she communicates in a dysfunctional way, she might say any of the following things:

   > "You would like to see a movie, <u>wouldn't</u> you."
   > "It would do you good to see a movie."
   > "If you want to see a movie, we'll see one."
   > "We might as well see a movie. It's Saturday night."
   > "There's a new movie house down the street."
   > "My voices are ordering me to see a movie."

30. These are some of the covert ways in which this wife can request something from her husband without acknowledging that she is making a request.

   a. She does not clearly label her wish which is behind her request, as <u>her</u> wish.

   b. Or, she may fail to label her wish <u>as a wish.</u> It becomes not a wish but a "must," something one is commanded to do. (The commander may be the other person or people in general, or "one's duty" or "voices" or something foreign inside of the self.)

   c. Or, she may label her wish as not a wish but as "the lesser of two evils."

31. The husband, in this case, could do some checking out. He could say: "Do <u>you</u> want to see a movie?" or "Do you want to see a movie <u>with me</u>?"

   a. But here is what can happen if the husband does ask his wife what she meant by her communication. She might go on to explain her message in any one of the following statements:

   > "No, I thought <u>you</u> wanted to go."
   > "No, I just thought we <u>should.</u>"
   > "No, I don't necessarily want to go. I want to do what you want."
   > "There are times when I want to see a movie, but this isn't one of them."

"I don't particularly want to go. My voices are ordering me."

32. By denying that she had a wish, the wife is also denying that her wish was expressed toward her husband. She denies that she has made a request of him. If he pursues his questions, she may go on to deny further.

> "You can go or not. I don't care."
> "If you want to be a stay-at-home, that's your business.'
> "If you go to the movies, you go to the movies."
> "Nobody asked you to go. If you want to go, then go."

33. The wife, when replying to her husband's request (in this case, a request to clarify), denies any or all parts of her message.

   a. The Bateson group, and Jay Haley, in particular, has defined four parts of every message:
   -- I (the sender)
   -- am saying something (message)
   -- to you (the receiver)
   -- in this situation (context). (109)
   b. All messages are requests, yet the wife may deny this, in so many words, by saying:

   > "I didn't care one way or the other." (I didn't request anything.)
   > "I just threw out a suggestion for whatever it was worth." (I didn't request anything.)
   > "Whether or not you go to the movies is immaterial to me." (I didn't request anything of you.)
   > "At one time, I might have wanted to go with you. But I know better now." (I didn't request anything of you just now.)

34. We note how defensive the wife is, as she sends her highly incomplete message. (These messages are incomplete because they do not clearly label "I, want this, from you, in this situation.") She makes it hard for her husband to find out what she wants.

   a. She covers herself as she sends her request, almost as though she anticipated refusal.

   > "Voices are ordering me..."
   > "I am doing this for you..."
   > "There's a new movie house down the street."

    b. She covers herself after she is asked to clarify: "I thought <u>you</u> wanted me to go," or, "Nobody asked you to go."

35. We also note how offensive the wife is, as she sends her request and responds to requests to clarify. She makes it hard for her husband to want to do what she wants.

    a. She disparages him in anticipation of refusal:

> "A person should see a movie at least once a month if he professes to be cultured."
> "We might as well see a movie. I'm bored."

    b. She disparages him after he asks her to clarify (and this very disparagement reveals her disappointment over the fact that he does not seem influenceable):

> "I can't <u>make</u> you do anything."
> "You'll do exactly what you <u>feel</u> like doing."
> "Ask anything of you? I know better!"

36. One could decide, on first thought, that this wife is a dysfunctional communicator and that she puts unnecessary burdens on her functional husband who, in this case, tries to check out the meaning of her message.

    a. But when people communicate, they are sending a message to a receiver.
    b. The wife tailors her message to the way she thinks her husband will respond to it.
    c. Once we note how he does respond to her, we will see that her messages are tailored to a kind of response which she has learned to expect from her husband.
    d. Her husband, in his response, does the same.

37. One cannot view messages separate from interaction, as I have been doing, and receive the full picture.

    a. One must at least note what A says, how B responds, how A responds to B's response. Communication is a two-sided affair; senders are receivers, receivers are also senders.
    b. One must note whether or not these interaction sequences repeat themselves over time and in different content areas.
    c. If they do repeat themselves, these sequences represent how these two people characteristically communicate with one another.

38. However, before analyzing interaction, one can profit from analyzing isolated messages. Such an analysis:

 a. Highlights different principles about messages and message-
 sending.
 b. Highlights the kinds of problems which highly defensive communication poses for the receiver.
 c. Helps document inferences about what inner wishes and fears
 dictate and how they perpetuate dysfunctional communication.

39. This husband's communication does have something to do with the
wife's characteristic way of asking for something from him.

 a. But even before analyzing this, we can guess that this wife
 fears that her husband will reject her request.
 b. Behind her denials that she has a wish and has made a request,
 is the wish that her husband would not only want to go to the
 movies with her, but would want to do what she wants because
 he loves her: "You'll do what you _feel_ like doing".
 c. She is not unusual in having this want. But if she cannot come
 to terms with it, she can easily trap herself and her husband
 in an impossible dilemma.
 -- No two people think alike on everything.
 -- No two people feel the same way at all times within a relationship.
 -- No two people want the same things or want them at the
 same time. People operate from different timetables.
 -- We are, in fact, autonomous, different, and unique beings.
 -- Yet we are, at the same time, dependent on others. We need
 them to help us get many of the things we want (or not pre-
 vent us from getting them). We are also dependent on others
 to validate our existence and worth.

40. Therefore, even though people are making requests of others
when they communicate, there are some things that cannot be
requested. Yet these are the very things people also want.

 a. We cannot ask that others feel as we do or as we want them
 to. As Bateson and Watzlawick have pointed out, feelings are
 spontaneous; they are not subject to self-request or to the requests of others. (20, 256)
 -- All we can do is try to elicit feelings.
 -- Failing to elicit, we can accept our disappointment and try
 again.
 b. We cannot ask that others think as we do. Thoughts are not

subject to the requests of others.

-- All we can do is try to persuade others, and present our arguments in the clearest, most cogent form possible.

-- Failing to persuade, we can accept our disappointment and compromise, or "agree to disagree."

c. We can, of course, <u>demand</u> that others say or do (or not say or not do) what we want. But if we succeed in this, our success will be questionable.

-- We shall have validated our power but not our lovability or worth, since we have "had to ask."

-- Also, since such a tactic challenges the other's autonomy, it is likely that he will feel devalued and will devalue back.

41. Evidently man is insatiable. He can never be loved enough, valued enough. Yet he can never be safe enough, powerful enough.

a. These two wants are contradictory if viewed on the same continuum. Man seems to have a built-in potential for defeating himself.

-- If he sees these two wants as an either/or proposition, he puts them in conflict with each other and loses out on both.

-- If he allows them to coexist, each in its proper time and place, he will not only gain both, but will find that each enhances the other.

b. The way he communicates with other persons will take its form from whichever of these two approaches he adopts.

-- If he takes the first approach, it indicates that he will handle the different-ness of others in terms of <u>war</u> and <u>who is right</u>.

-- If he takes the second, he will handle different-ness on the basis of <u>exploration</u> and <u>what fits</u>.

-- The former leads to stalemating, retardation and pathology.

-- The latter leads to growth, individuality and creativity.

c. In the next chapter, I shall be going into this question of how dysfunctional and functional communication express and influence pathology and health.

PART THREE: THEORY AND PRACTICE OF THERAPY

Chapter X

Concepts of Therapy

1. In this chapter, I should like to restate in a more general way
   some of the ideas about psychic health and illness which we have
   discussed previously, in order to show their relevance to the interactional approach of family therapy. I also want to present
   my own picture of what a family therapist is and does, since he
   becomes, to an important degree, a model for his patients' subsequent behavior.

   I am not trying to present a "philosophy of therapy." These ideas
   appear to me as working tools, helpful in organizing my own way
   of handling therapy, or as a conceptual core around which therapeutic growths may be structured, rather than as a system of
   thought possessing value in and for itself.

   Finally, let me say that this discussion of theory is admittedly
   schematic, not filled in. I intend to follow this volume with a
   later one in which I will be illustrating my basis of operations
   more fully with examples from actual family situations.

2. The most important concept in therapy, because it is a touchstone
   for all the rest, is that of <u>maturation.</u>

   a. This is the state in which a given human being is fully in charge
      of himself.
   b. A mature person is one who, having attained his majority, is
      able to make choices and decisions based on accurate percep-
      tions about himself, others, and the context in which he finds
      himself; who acknowledges these choices and decisions as be-
      ing his; and who accepts responsibility for their outcomes.

3. The patterns of behaving that characterize a mature person we
   call functional because they enable him to deal in a relatively

competent and precise way with the world in which he lives. Such a person will:

a. manifest himself clearly to others.
b. be in touch with signals from his internal self, thus letting himself know openly what he thinks and feels.
c. be able to see and hear what is outside himself as differentiated from himself and as different from anything else.
d. behave toward another person as someone separate from himself and unique.
e. treat the presence of different-ness as an opportunity to learn and explore rather than as a threat or a signal for conflict.
f. deal with persons and situations in their context, in terms of "how it is" rather than how he wishes it were or expects it to be.
g. accept responsibility for what he feels, thinks, hears and sees, rather than denying it or attributing it to others.
h. have techniques for openly negotiating the giving, receiving and checking of meaning between himself and others. *

4. We call an individual dysfunctional when he has not learned to communicate properly. Since he does not manifest a means of perceiving and interpreting himself accurately, or interpreting accurately messages from the outside, the assumptions on which he bases his actions will be faulty and his efforts to adapt to reality will be confused and inappropriate.

a. As we have seen, the individual's communication problems are rooted in the complex area of family behavior in which he lived as a child. The adults in the family provide the blueprint by which the child grows from infancy to maturity.
b. If the male and female who were his survival figures did not manage jointly, if their messages to each other and the child were unclear and contradictory, he himself will learn to communicate in an unclear and contradictory way.

5. A dysfunctional person will manifest himself incongruently, that is, he will deliver conflicting messages, via different levels of communication and using different signals.

a. As an example, let us take the behavior of the parents of a disturbed child during their first interview with the therapist. When the therapist asks what seems to be the trouble, they practically deny that there is any.

> M: Well, I don't know. I think financial problems more than anything... outside of that, we're a very close family.

---

*This description of maturity emphasizes social and communication skills rather than the acquisition of knowledge and recognized achievement, which in my view derive from the first two.

F: We do everything together. I mean, we hate to leave the kids. When we go someplace, we take the kids with us. As far as doing things together as a family, we always try to do that at least once a week, say on Sundays, Sunday afternoon, why we always try to get the kids together and take them out for a ride to the park or something like that.

b. In words, they imply that there is no reason why they should be in a therapist's office. But their actual presence there, and the agreement they have already made to enter therapy, amount to an admission of the contrary. And the father presents a further contradiction when he reduces his claim that the family does "everything" together to a statement about the rides they take on Sunday afternoons.

6. In addition, a dysfunctional individual will be unable to adapt his interpretations to the present context.

a. He will tend to see the "here and now" through labels which have been indelibly fixed in his mind during the early part of his life when all messages had survival significance. Each subsequent use of the label will strengthen its reality.

b. Therefore, it is conceivable that he will impose on the present that which fits the past, or that which he expects from the future, thus negating the opportunity to gain a perspective on the past or realistically shape the future.
   -- For example, a school-age girl was brought into therapy because she was acting strangely and talking in riddles. When the mother was asked, "When did you notice that your child was not developing as she should?" she replied, "Well, she was a seven-month baby, and she was in an incubator for six weeks." The child's present and past difficulties were thus connected in a very illogical fashion. *
   -- Later she said that after she brought the baby home from the hospital, "She wouldn't give me any reaction, just as though she couldn't hear. And I'd take her around and hold her next to me, and she wouldn't pay any attention, and I know it upset me, and I asked the doctor and he said it was nothing, she was just being stubborn— that's one thing that sort of stuck in my mind with her."
   -- By using the word "stubborn" for the baby's indifference, the mother has given the baby a label that does not suit the

---

*The communication aspects of this situation Jackson has labeled "past-present switches." Thus, the answer to the therapist's question, "How out of all the millions of people in the world did you two find each other?" may be as useful in family diagnosis as psychological testing. This question allows the spouses to describe their present relationship under cover of talking about the past. For further examples of this phenomenon, see Watzlawick's *An Anthology of Human Communication*. (256)

context of babyhood. It implies that the child can be held accountable for willfully refusing to return the mother's love. Later on, the mother applies the same explanation to the child's strange behavior.

-- By using the label "stubborn," and by implying in her first statement that the child's difficulties have a physical cause, the mother is able to absolve herself of blame; in fact, she has a double coverage. It is hard for such a mother to see her child's present problems objectively because she has already imposed her own interpretation on them.

7. Finally, a dysfunctional individual will not be able to perform the most important function of good communication: "checking out" his perceptions to see whether they tally with the situation as it really is or with the intended meaning of another. When two people are neither of them able to check out their meanings with each other, the result may resemble a comedy of errors -- with a tragic ending. Here is one possible misunderstanding between a husband and a wife:

Report: W: "He always yells." H: "I don't yell."

Explanation: W: "I don't do things to suit him." H: "I don't do things to suit her."

Interpretation: W: "He doesn't care about me." H: "She doesn't care about me."

Conclusion: W: "I will leave him." H: "I will leave her."

Manifestation: Wife uses invectives, voice is loud and shrill, eyes blaze, muscles stand out on base of neck, mouth is open, nostrils are distended, uses excessive movements. Husband says nothing, keeps eyes lowered, mouth tight, body constricted.

Outcome: Wife visits divorce lawyer. Husband files a counter-suit.

8. Difficulty in communicating is closely linked to an individual's self-concept, that is, his self-image and self-esteem.

a. His parents may not only have given him inadequate models for _methods_ of communication, but the _content_ of their messages to him may have been devaluating (see Chapter VI).

b. In order to form his self-image, the child has a demanding task. He must integrate messages from both parents (separately and together) telling him what to do with aspects of living like dependency, authority, sexuality and coding or labeling (cognition).

c. If the parents' own attitudes are uncertain, or if they disagree with each other, the messages the child takes will be equally confused. The child will try to integrate what cannot be inte-- grated, on the basis of inconsistent and insufficient data. Failing, he will end up with an incomplete picture of himself and low self-esteem.

d. In addition, the child's parents may depreciate his self-esteem more directly. He looks to them to validate his steps in growth; if these are not acknowledged at the time they occur, or if they are acknowledged with concomitant messages of disgust, disapproval, embarrassment, indifference or pain, the child's self-esteem will naturally suffer.

9. Low self-esteem leads to dysfunctional communication:

a. When there is a conflict of interests. Any relationship presupposes a commitment to a joint outcome, an agreement that each partner will give up a little of his own interests in order to reach a wider benefit for both.
-- This outcome is the best objective reality that can be arrived at in terms of what is possible, what is feasible, what fits the best all the way around.
-- The process used for reaching this outcome depends on the self-concepts of the persons engaged in it. If their self-esteem is low, so that any sacrifice of self seems intolererable, it is likely that the process will be based on some form of deciding "who is right," "who will win," "who is most loved," "who will get mad." I call this the "war syndrome."
-- If a person operates by means of this war syndrome, it is inevitable that his ability to seek objective information and arrive at objective conclusions as to what fits will be greatly impaired.

b. Dysfunction in communication will also follow when the individual is unable to handle different-ness.
-- As we have seen in Chapter III, an individual who has not achieved an independent selfhood will often take any evidence of different-ness in someone he is close to as an insult or a sign of being unloved.
-- This is because he is intensely dependent on the other person to increase his feelings of worth and to validate his self-image. Any reminder that the other is, after all, a separate being, capable of faithlessness and desertion, fills him with fear and distrust.
-- Some couples express their objections to each other's different-ness freely and loudly (see the "teeter-totter syndrome," page 17), but others, less secure in this area, prefer to pretend that different-ness does not exist.
-- With such couples, communication becomes covert (see page 15). Any message which might call attention to the self as a private agent, with likes and dislikes, desires and displeasures of its own, is suppressed or changed.

Wishes and decisions are presented as if they emanated from anywhere but inside the speaker himself; statements are disguised as symbolic utterances; messages are left incomplete or even not expressed at all, with the sender relying on mental telepathy to get them across (see pages 86-88). For example, a couple who overtly behaved as if they had absolutely no problems responded in therapy to the "How did you meet?" question as follows:

> H: "Well, we were raised in the same neighborhood."

> W: "Not exactly the same neighborhood" (laughs).

This slight modification on the wife's part presaged many revelations of serious division between them.

10. Thus far we have been talking about dysfunctional behavior rather than the symptom that calls attention to it. What is the connection between them?

    a. Dysfunctional behavior is, as we have seen, related to feelings of low self-esteem. It is, in fact, a defense against the perception of them. Defenses, in turn, are ways which enable the person with low self-esteem to function without a symptom. To the person himself and to the outward world, there may appear to be nothing wrong.

    b. But if he is threatened by some event of survival significance, some happening which says to him, "You do not count; you are not lovable; you are nothing," the defense may prove unequal to the task of shielding him, and a symptom will take its place.

    c. Usually it is only then that the individual and his community will notice that he is "ill" and that he will admit a need for help.

11. How, then, do we define therapy?

    a. If illness is seen to derive from inadequate methods of communication (by which we mean all interactional behavior), it follows that therapy will be seen as an attempt to improve these methods. As will be seen in the chapters on therapy, the emphasis will be on correcting discrepancies in communication and teaching ways to achieve more fitting joint outcomes.

    b. This approach to therapy depends on three primary beliefs about human nature:

      -- First, that every individual is geared to survival, growth, and getting close to others and that all behavior expresses these aims, no matter how distorted it may look. Even an extremely disturbed person will be fundamentally on the side of the therapist.

      -- Second, that what society calls sick, crazy, stupid, or bad behavior is really an attempt on the part of the afflicted person to signal the presence of trouble and call for help. In that sense, it may not be so sick, crazy, stupid, or bad after all.

-- Third, that human beings are limited only by the extent of their knowledge, their ways of understanding themselves and their ability to "check out" with others. Thought and feeling are inextricably bound together; the individual need not be a prisoner of his feelings but can use the cognitive component of his feeling to free himself. This is the basis for assuming that a human being can learn what he doesn't know and can change ways of commenting and understanding that don't fit.

12. This brings us to a discussion of the role of the therapist. How will he act? What picture will he have of himself?

    a. Perhaps the best way that he can see himself is as a <u>resource person</u>. He is not omnipotent. He is not God, parent or judge. The knotty question for all therapists is how to be an expert without appearing to the patient to be all-powerful, omniscient, or presuming to know always what is right and wrong.

    b. The therapist does have a special advantage in being able to study the patient's family situation as an experienced observer, while remaining outside it, above the power struggle, so to speak. Like a camera with a wide-angle lens, he can see things from the position of each person present and act as a representative of each. He sees transactions, as well as the individuals involved, and thus has a unique viewpoint.

    c. Because of this, the family can place their trust in him as an "official observer," one who can report impartially on what he sees and hears. Above all, he can report on what the family cannot see and cannot report on.

13. The therapist must also see himself as a <u>model of communication.</u>

    a. First of all, he must take care to be aware of his own prejudices and unconscious assumptions so as not to fall into the trap he warns others about, that of suiting reality to himself. His lack of fear in revealing himself may be the first experience the family has had with clear communication.

    b. In addition, the way he interprets and structures the action of therapy from the start is the first step in introducing the family to new techniques in communication.

    c. Here is an example of how the therapist clarifies the process of interaction for a family:

        Th: (to husband) I notice your brow is wrinkled, Ralph. Does that mean you are angry at this moment?

        H: I did not know that my brow was wrinkled.

Th: Sometimes a person looks or sounds in a way of which he is not aware. As far as you can tell, what were you thinking and feeling just now?

H: I was thinking over what she (his wife) said.

Th: What thing that she said were you thinking about?

H: When she said that when she was talking so loud, she wished I would tell her.

Th: What were you thinking about that?

H: I never thought about telling her. I thought she would get mad.

Th: Ah, then maybe that wrinkle meant you were puzzled because your wife was hoping you would do something and you did not know she had this hope. Do you suppose that by your wrinkled brow you were signalling that you were puzzled?

H: Yeh, I guess so.

Th: As far as you know, have you ever been in that same spot before, that is, where you were puzzled by something Alice said or did?

H: Hell, yes, lots of times.

Th: Have you ever told Alice you were puzzled when you were?

W: He never says anything.

Th: (smiling, to Alice) Just a minute, Alice, let me hear what Ralph's idea is of what he does. Ralph, how do you think you have let Alice know when you are puzzled?

H: I think she knows.

Th: Well, let's see. Suppose you ask Alice if she knows.

H: This is silly.

Th: (smiling) I suppose it might seem so in this situation, because Alice is right here and certainly has heard what your question is. She knows what it is. I have the suspicion, though, that neither you nor Alice are very sure about what the other expects, and I think you have not developed ways to find out. Alice, let's go back to when I commented on Ralph's wrinkled brow. Did you happen to notice it, too?

W: (complaining) Yes, he always looks like that.

Th: What kind of a message did you get from that wrinkled brow?

W: He don't want to be here. He don't care. He never talks. Just looks at television or he isn't home.

Th: I'm curious. Do you mean that when Ralph has a wrinkled brow that you take this as Ralph's way of saying, "I don't love you, Alice. I don't care about you, Alice."?

W: (exasperated and tearfully) I don't know.

Th: Well, maybe the two of you have not yet worked out crystal-clear ways of giving your love and value messages to each other. Everyone needs crystal-clear ways of giving their value messages. (to son) What do you know, Jim, about how you give your value messages to your parents?

S: I don't know what you mean.

Th: Well, how do you let your mother, for instance, know that you like her, when you are feeling that way. Everyone feels different ways at different times. When you are feeling glad your mother is around, how do you let her know?

S: I do what she tells me to do. Work and stuff.

Th: I see, so when you do your work at home, you mean this for a message to your mother that you're glad she is around.

S: Not exactly.

Th: You mean you are giving a different message then. Well, Alice, did you take this message from Jim to be a love message? (to Jim) What do you do to give your father a message that you like him?

S: (after a pause) I can't think of nothin'.

Th: Let me put it another way. What do you know crystal-clear that you could do that would bring a smile to your father's face?

S: I could get better grades in school.

Th: Let's check this out and see if you are perceiving clearly. Do you, Alice, get a love message from Jim when he works around the house?

W: I s'pose -- he doesn't do very much.

Th: So from where you sit, Alice, you don't get many love messages from Jim. Tell me, Alice, does Jim have any other ways that he might not now be thinking about that he has that say to you that he is glad you are around?

W: (softly) The other day he told me I looked nice.

Th: What about you, Ralph, does Jim perceive correctly that if he got better grades you would smile?

H: I don't imagine I will be smiling for some time.

Th: I hear that you don't think he is getting good grades, but would you smile if he did?

H: Sure, hell, I would be glad.

Th: As you think about it, how do you suppose you would show it?

W: You never know if you ever please him.

Th: We have already discovered that you and Ralph have not yet developed crystal-clear ways of showing value feelings toward one another. Maybe you, Alice, are now observing this between Jim and Ralph. What do think, Ralph? Do you suppose it would be hard for Jim to find out when he has pleased you?

14. The therapist will not only exemplify what he means by clear communication, but he will teach his patients how to achieve it themselves.

a. He will spell out the rules for communication accurately. In particular, he will emphasize the necessity for checking out meaning given with meaning received. He will see that the patient keeps in mind the following complicated set of mirror images:
-- Self's idea (how I see me).
-- Self's idea of other (how I see you).
-- Self's idea of other's idea of self (how I see you seeing me).
-- Self's idea of other's idea of self's idea of other (how I

see you seeing me seeing you).
Only if a person is able to check back and forth across the
lines of communication, can he be sure that he has completed
a clear exchange.

b. The therapist will help the patient to be aware of messages
that are incongruent, confused or covert (see pages 175-176
for examples).

c. At the same time, the therapist will show the patient how to
check on invalid assumptions that are used as fact. He knows
that members of dysfunctional families are afraid to question
each other to find out what each really means. They seem to
say to each other: "I can't let you know what I see and hear
and think and feel or you will drop dead, attack or desert me."
As a result, each operates from his assumptions, which he
takes from the other person's manifestations and thereupon
treats as fact. The therapist uses various questions to ferret
out these invalid assumptions, such as:

> "What did you say? What did you hear me say?"

> "What did you see or hear that led you to make that
> conclusion?"

> "What message did you intend to get across?"

> "If I had been there, what would I have seen or heard?"

> "How do you know? How can you find out?"

> "You look calm, but how do you feel in the stomach?"

d. Like any good teacher, the therapist will try to be crystal-
clear.
-- He will repeat, restate and emphasize his own observations,
sometimes to the point of seeming repetitious and simple.
He will do the same with observations made by members
of the family.
-- He will also be careful to give his reasons for arriving at
any conclusion. If the patient is baffled by some statement
of the therapist's and does not know the reasoning behind
it, this will only increase his feelings of powerlessness.

15. The therapist will be aware of the many possibilities of interaction in therapy.

a. In the therapeutic situation, the presence of the therapist
adds as many dyads (two-person systems) as there are people in the family, since he relates to each member. The therapist, like the other people present, operates as a member of
various dyads but also as the observer of other dyads. These

shifts of position could be confusing to him and to the family.
If, for example, he has taken someone's part, he should
clearly state he is doing so.

b. The therapist clarifies the nature of interchanges made during therapy, but he has to select those that are representative
since he can't possibly keep up with everything that is said.
Luckily, family sequences are apt to be redundant, so one
clarification may serve a number of exchanges.

c. Here is an illustration of the way the therapist isolates and
underlines each exchange.

-- When the therapist states, "When you, Ralph, said you were
angry, I noticed that you, Alice, had a frown on your face,"
this is an example of the therapist reporting himself as a
monad ("I see you, Alice; I hear you, Ralph"), and reporting
to Ralph and Alice as monads (the use of the word you, followed by the specific name). Then, by the therapist's use
of the word when, he establishes that there is a connection
between the husband's report and the wife's report, thus
validating the presence of an interaction.

-- If the therapist then turns to the oldest son, Jim, and says,
"What do you, Jim, make of what just happened between
your mother and father?" the therapist is establishing Jim
as an observer, since family members may forget that they
monitor each other's behavior.

-- When Jim answers, everyone knows what his perception is.
If it turns out that Jim's report does not fit what either
Alice or Ralph intended, then there is an opportunity to
find out what was intended, what was picked up by Jim, and
why he interpreted it that way.

16. Labeling an illness is a part of therapy that a therapist must approach with particular care.

a. A therapist, when he deals with a patient, is confronting a
person who has been labeled by others or by himself as having
emotional, physical or social disorders. To the non-therapeu-
tic observer, the behavior which signals the presence of a dis-
order is usually labeled "stupid," "crazy," "sick" or "bad."

b. The therapist will use other labels, like "mentally defective,"
"underachieving," "schizophrenic," "manic-depressive,"
"psychosomatic," "sociopathic." These are labels used by
clinicians to describe behavior which is seen to be deviant:
deviant from the rest of the person's character, deviant from
the expectation of others, and deviant from the context in
which the person finds himself.

c. The observations made by clinicians over the years have been
brought together under a standardized labeling system called
the "psychiatric nomenclature." It is a method of shorthand
used by clinicians to describe deviant behavior.

d. These labels often presuppose an exact duplication of all the
individuals so labeled. Over the years, each of the labels has

been given an identity, with prognosis and treatment implications based on the dimensions of that identity.

e. If a therapist has labeled a person "schizophrenic," for instance, he may have based his prognosis of that person on his ideas about schizophrenia, rather than on an observation of a person who, among other labels like "human being," "Jim," "husband," "father," "chemist," has the label "schizophrenic."

f. But neither the clinician or any other person has the right to treat him only in terms of the label "schizophrenic" while losing sight of him as a total human being. No label is infallible, because no diagnosis is, but by identifying the person with the label, the therapist shuts his mind to the possibility of different interpretations which different evidence might point to.

g. The therapist must say to his patient, in effect: You are behaving now with behavior which I, as a clinician, label "schizophrenia." But this label only applies <u>at this time</u>, <u>in this place</u>, and <u>in this context</u>. Future times, places and contexts may show something quite different.

17. Let us close this discussion of the role of the therapist with a look at some of the specific advantages family therapy will have compared to individual or group therapy.

a. In family therapy, the therapist will have a greater opportunity to observe objectively. In individual therapy, since there are only two people, the therapist is part of the interaction. It is hard for him to be impartial. In addition, he must sift out the patient's own reactions and feelings from those which might be a response to clues from the therapist himself.

b. The family therapist will be able to get firsthand knowledge of the patient in two important areas.
   -- By observing the individual in his family, the therapist can see where he is in terms of his present level of growth.
   -- By observing a child in the family group, the therapist can find out how his functioning came to be handicapped. He can see for himself how the husband and wife relate to each other and how they relate to the child.
   -- This kind of firsthand knowledge is not possible in individual therapy, or even in group therapy, where the individual is with members of his peer group and the kind of interaction that can be studied is limited to this single aspect.

18. As a therapist, I have found certain concepts useful, somewhat like measuring tools, in determining the nature and extent of dysfunction in a family.

a. I make an analysis of the techniques used by each member of the family for <u>handling the presence of different-ness</u>. A person's reaction to different-ness is an index to his ability to adapt to growth and change. It also indicates what attitudes he will have toward other members of his family, and whether he will be able to express these attitudes directly or not.

-- The members of any family need to have ways to find out about and make room for their different-ness. This requires that each can report directly what he perceives about himself and the other, to himself and to the other.

-- Example: Janet misses her hatpin. She must say, "I need my hatpin (clear), which I am telling you, Betty, about, (direct), and it is the hatpin that I use for the only black hat I have (specific)." Not: "Why don't you leave my hat alone?" or "Isn't there something you want to tell me?" or going into Betty's room and turning things upsidedown (unclear, indirect, and unspecific).

-- As I have said before, when one of the partners in a marriage is confronted with a different-ness in the other that he did not expect, or that he did not know about, it is important that he treat this as an opportunity to explore and to understand rather than as a signal for war.

-- If the techniques for handling different-ness are based on determining who is right (war), or pretending that the different-ness does not exist (denial), then there is a potential for pathological behavior on the part of any member of the family, but particularly the children.

b. I make what I call a role function analysis to find out whether the members of a family are covertly playing roles different from those which their position in the family demands that they play (see page 174).

-- If two people have entered a marriage with the hope of extending the self, each is in effect put in charge of the other, thus creating a kind of mutual parasitic relationship.

-- This relationship will eventually be translated into something that looks like a parent-child relationship. The adults, labeled "husband" and "wife," may in reality be functioning as mother and son, father and daughter, or as siblings, to the confusion of the rest of the family and, ultimately, themselves.

-- Here is an oversimplified example of the way things might go in such a family:

> Suppose Mary takes over the role of sole parent, with Joe acting the part of her child. Joe then takes the part of a brother to their two children, John and Patty, and becomes a rival with them for their mother's affections. To handle his rivalry and prove his place, he may start drinking excessively, or he may bury himself in his work in order to avoid coming home. Mary, deserted, may turn to John in such a way as to make him feel he must take his father's place. Wishing to do so but in reality unable to, John may become delinquent, turning against his mother and choosing some-

one on the outside. Or he may accept his mother's invitation, which would be to give up being male and become homosexual. Patty may regress or remain infantile to keep her place. Joe may get ulcers. Mary may become psychotic.

  -- These are only some of the possibilities for disturbance in a family that has become dislocated by incongruent role-playing.

c. I make a <u>self-manifestation</u> <u>analysis</u> for each member of a family. If what a person says does not fit with the way he looks, sounds and acts, or if he reports his wishes and feelings as belonging to someone else or as coming from somewhere else, I know that he will not be able to produce reliable clues for any other person interacting with him. When such behavior, which I call "<u>manifesting incongruency,</u>" is present in the members of a family to any large degree, there will be a potential for development of pathology.

d. In order to find out how the early life of each member of a family has affected his present ways of behaving, I make what I call a <u>model</u> <u>analysis</u> (see pages 173-174).

  -- This means that I try to discover who the models were (or are) that influenced each family member in his early life; who gave him messages about the presence and desirability of growth; who gave him the blueprint from which he learned to evaluate and act on new experience; who showed him how to become close to others.

  -- Because these messages have survival significance, the ways in which they are given will automatically determine the way the individual interprets later messages from other adults, who may not be survival-connected but who may be invested with survival significance, like spouses, in-laws or bosses. *

19. The ideas in this chapter have been discussed out of the context of ongoing therapy, where they belong. In the next three chapters, I hope to show very specifically how I, as a therapist, incorporate them into the action of therapy, from the first time I see a family to the termination of treatment.

---

*While there are obvious connections between this theory and both the analytic concept of transference and the Sullivanian concept of parataxic distortion, there are also differences. In particular, instead of inferring from the transference the probable nature of the individual's early environment, I use the information about his past to evaluate the survival significance of his current messages.

Chapter XI

Opening Treatment

1. In this last part, I should like to go behind scenes and describe in detail the techniques I have found most useful in practicing family therapy. Although I naturally believe in my own methods, and hope that others may find it helpful to read about them, I do not mean to imply that they are the last and only word in therapeutic procedure.

   This is because I feel strongly that each therapist must find his unique and individual way of practicing his craft. When he deals with patients, he should never sacrifice his particular flavor to some kind of professional, impersonal ideal. As you will see, wherever I could I have kept my own style of phrasing things (like asking "What hurts?" of a family), my favorite idioms and ways of joking.

   I have also found that an informal and individual manner helps to keep a therapeutic interview from resembling a funeral rite or a courtroom scene, and establishes an atmosphere which encourages hopefulness and good will.

   In this section I have included examples of the kind of questions that I use to draw people out and make them aware of their own communication. These may seem unnecessarily repetitious and simple at times, or even as if the therapist were hard of hearing. However, we must remember that when we are dealing with more than one person, and when these persons do not yet know how to say what they mean, or to ask what others mean, this repetitiousness and simplifying is a central part of the therapeutic process. It is often astonishing to an inexperienced therapist how frequently family members cannot ask even simple, fact-finding questions of each other and must be shown how.

   Another reason for asking so many questions and repeating them for each person in the family, is to give the other persons present a new and perhaps enlightening perspective on the way things look, or looked, to the speaker.

2. Let us start now with the first contact the therapist has with a family member, which will probably be a telephone call. In this first contact, the therapist will concentrate on four things:

a. He will try to find out who makes up the Jones family.
   -- For example, does Johnny have brothers or sisters? If so, how old are they? Does grandmother live right around the corner? If so, how often is she involved in family life?
   -- Has anyone recently moved in or out of the family? If so, who? Grandfather? A new baby? A boarder?
b. He will try to find out the ages of family members, because such information tells him where all members are expected to be in their chronological maturity. It also tells him what kind of parenting load the mates have to carry.
   -- For example, are Mary and her husband, Joe, in their twenties, thirties, fifties? Is this a young or an older family?
   -- How old is Johnny? Where is he now in his growth toward maturity? (The therapist may not find out all these things in the first contact, but he keeps these questions in mind as he talks to Mary Jones on the phone.)
c. He introduces Mary Jones to the family therapy approach, making it clear to her that it is important that her husband take part in the therapy.
d. Initially, he talks to Mary about herself and Joe as parents of Johnny, rather than as mates to each other. In this way he joins temporarily in their focus on Johnny as the problem; as "the reason why we have decided to ask for help."
e. Here is an example of a first contact on the phone:

W: This is Mrs. Jones. I have heard about this idea of family therapy and wondered if you could help us.

Th: What seems to be the problem?

W: Well, we are having problems with my boy, Johnny. He is not doing at all well in school. As a matter of fact he... he has not been a very difficult child at all up to now. But he has this new teacher who has been pretty hard on him. I don't know. He just won't behave, and we have received several complaints from the school. They say he is quite tense, and I guess he is...

Th: I see. The teachers have complained about Johnny's behavior in school. He is tense. How does he show this? How do they say he shows this?

W: Well, he cuts up a good deal and won't settle down, and they say he is hard to handle. I just don't understand it. Frankly, I'm at my wits' end. He won't tell me what is wrong, and I thought maybe if you would... if there is something we are doing wrong...

Th: It certainly sounds as if things aren't going as you hoped. We can look at this and see how it came about and try to understand it better.

W: Well, we have done everything we could. We have given him everything a child could want.

Th: I'm sure this has been confusing to you, and you are trying hard to make some sense ot it. As you know, we do family work here, and I think we should start out with you and your husband. I think that would be best. You are the adults in the family. Tell me, who is in your family?

W: Well, there's Johnny and Patty. And my husband, Joe, and me. Just four of us.

Th: There are four of you. Your husband's name is Joe. And Johnny and Patty, what are their ages?

W: Johnny is ten. Patty is going on seven.

Th: Johnny is ten. Patty is almost seven. Anyone else in the family?

W: No.

Th: Well, as I said, we do family work here. So we should start out with the two adults. I would be happy to make an appointment for you and your husband. Then later we can see about bringing the children in.

W: Well, I...well, I'm not sure. Joe would...I'm not sure he would want to do that. I haven't asked him but he's...

Th: We need information from your husband that only he can give. It is very important that I see you both. Tell your husband that a family is not a family without the father and the mother present. It is very important that we have the opportunity to get his contributions on this.

W: Well, I'll tell him. But I don't know. He's pretty...he's not too sympathetic...He's, uh...

Th: Tell your husband that we need his contributions. We

need to get his view of the situation as the male adult
in the family. We need all the information we can get,
and a father's contributions are very important. Only
he can speak for himself. No one else can give what
he can give.

W: Well, I'll try. When could you see us?

Joe will come in with his wife for the first appointment. Rarely,
with this kind of approach, does the husband, in his role of
father, fail to respond. The therapist's emphasis seems to
give the husband a new importance in the wife's eyes.

3. In the first interview, the therapist will start out by asking
   questions to establish what the family wants and expects from
   treatment.

   a. He will ask each person present, though not necessarily in
      these words:

      "How did you happen to come here?"

      "What do you expect will happen here?"

      "What do you hope to accomplish here."

   b. The therapist will then explain the nature of family therapy. He
      may say:

      "Families operate by rules which they may not even know
      about. I want to know about the operation of this family."

      "Each member of a family has to do something when he sees
      the presence of pain in another member. I need to find out
      what each of you does."

      "No one person can see the whole picture because he is lim-
      ited to his own perspective. By having everyone together we
      can get the whole picture more clearly. Every person has a
      unique contribution to make which cannot be duplicated by
      anyone else."

   c. The therapist will then ask each member of the family some
      questions for finding out about the symptom and its meaning
      such as:

      "Tell me, what do you see as the pain in this family?"

      "Anyone with a problem has pain in some way. Can you
      tell me where the pain is?"

"What 'hurts' in this family?"

Any one of these questions introduces the idea that the family, as a family, does have pain. It starts to shift the focus from the Identified Patient to the family as a whole. Each family member has a chance to identify, for himself, the problem area.

d. The parents usually answer that the Identified Patient is the problem and the therapist <u>briefly</u> orients himself to the problem as the parents see it:

"When did you first notice this symptom?"

"Did you discuss it between yourselves?"

"What steps did you take to try and relieve it?"

"What happened to these attempts?"

These questions allow the parents to tell how they have tried to be good parents and to present themselves accurately as puzzled. These questions also help the therapist get his first clues on several things: Who speaks for whom? Who makes the family rules? Who makes the plans? Who carries them out? How clearly are the plans communicated? Who speaks the most? Who speaks the least? What is the general pacing and tone of family communication? How clear and direct is family communication? How does the family respond to crises? In what area of behavior is the symptom manifested (I. Q., body, emotions, social)? What were the circumstances surrounding the onset of the symptom? What gap existed between onset and labeling of the symptom? Who (or what) has been blamed for the existence of the symptom (neighbors, teachers, God, heredity)? What purpose does the symptom serve in the family?

e. The therapist decreases threat of blame by accentuating the idea of puzzlement and the idea of good intentions:

"This must have puzzled you, that you did all these things and still nothing seemed to turn out as you hoped."

"We are all human. We do the best we can. It must have confused you when, with all these efforts, nothing seemed to go right."

f. The therapist then makes a bridge in order to cross over to beginning the family study. He may say:

"It sounds as though you have all been puzzled as to how

this difficulty of yours came to be."

"Once no one in this room knew each other. Maybe that time is hard to remember, and it may seem that you have always known each other. That is not so. You came together one by one. Each time another came, the others already there had to work out ways to make room for the new one."

"Now let's see who the persons are who have made up this family."

Chapter XII

Taking a Family Life Chronology

1. I almost always start family therapy (or even marital therapy) with what I call a "family life chronology" or history-taking process. Many therapists wonder why I do this.
   a. Doesn't such an approach lead the patient to tell the therapist what the therapist wants to know rather than encouraging the therapist to find out what the patient wants to tell him?
   b. Doesn't such an approach therefore violate our ideas about "self-determination"?
   c. Doesn't such an approach make the therapist too active in structuring the therapy process?

2. Ideas about how active a therapist should be and how much he should structure therapy have gone through a revolution since therapists started doing family therapy.

   a. Therapists who are new at family therapy have repeatedly discovered that if they do not intervene in family therapy sessions and stay active in them, the family will readily turn the therapist into a "fly on the wall," or "one of the family," or a "ping-pong ball."
   b. Regardless of the degree to which different therapists choose to structure their interventions, all family therapists soon realize that they cannot remain passive if they are going to be successful agents of change.

3. I recommend that the family therapist not only intervene in family therapy sessions but that he also structure at least the first two sessions by taking a family life chronology. I recommend this because:

   a. The family therapist enters a session knowing little or nothing about the family.
      -- He might know who the Identified Patient is and what symptoms he manifests, but that is usually all. So he must get clues about the meaning of the symptom.
      -- He might know that pain exists in the marital relationship but he needs to get clues about how the pain shows itself.

He needs to know how the mates have tried to cope with their problems.

-- He might know that the mates both operate from "models" (from what they saw going on between their own parents), but he needs to find out how these models have influenced each mate's expectations about how to be a mate and how to be a parent.

b. The family therapist enters a session knowing that the family has, in fact, had a history, but that is usually all he knows.

-- Every family, as a group, has gone through or jointly experienced many events. Certain events (such as deaths, childbirth, sickness, geographical moves, job changes) occur in almost all families.

-- Certain events primarily affected the mates and only indirectly the children. (Maybe the children weren't born yet or were too young to fully comprehend the nature of an event as it affected their parents. They might have only sensed periods of parental remoteness or distraction or anxiety or annoyance.)

-- The therapist can profit from answers to just about every question he asks.

c. Family members enter therapy with a great deal of fear. Therapist structuring helps decrease threat. It says: "I am in charge of what will happen here. I will see to it that nothing catastrophic happens here."

-- All members are covertly feeling very much to blame for the fact that nothing seems to have turned out right (even though they may overtly blame the Identified Patient or the other mate).

-- Parents, especially, need to feel that they did the best they could as parents. They need to tell the therapist: "This is why I did what I did. This is what happened to me."

-- A family life chronology which deals with facts such as names, dates, labeled relationships, moves, etc., seem to appeal to the family. It asks questions which members can answer, questions which are relatively nonthreatening. It deals with life as the family understands it.

d. Family members enter therapy with a great deal of despair. Therapist structuring helps stimulate hope.

-- As far as family members are concerned, past events are part of them. They now can tell the therapist: "I existed." And they can also tell him: "I am not just a big blob of pathology. I succeeded in overcoming many handicaps."

-- If the family knew what questions needed asking they wouldn't need to be in therapy. So the therapist does not say: "Tell me what you want to tell me." Family members will simply tell the therapist what they have been telling themselves for years. The therapist's questions say: "I know what to ask. I take responsibility for understanding you. We are going to go somewhere."

e. The family therapist also knows that, to some degree, the family has focused on an Identified Patient in order to relieve marital pain. He also knows that, to some degree, the family will resist any effort to change this focus. A family life chronology is an effective, nonthreatening way to change from an emphasis on the "sick" or "bad" family member to an emphasis on the marital relationship.

f. The family life chronology serves other useful therapy purposes, such as providing the framework within which a re-education process can take place. As we have said, the therapist serves as a model in the way he checks out information or corrects communication techniques, and the way he places his questions and elicits answers can allow him to begin this process. In addition, when he takes the chronology, he can introduce in a relatively nonfrightening way some of the crucial concepts by which he hopes to induce change.

4. From the family life chronology, the therapist gets his first clues as to how dysfunctional the marital relationship is.

a. If, for example, while answering the therapist's questions, the mates can readily talk about the pain in their own marital relationship, the prognosis for an early, successful outcome in therapy is good.

b. But if, during the chronology, the mates cannot readily talk about the marital relationship but insist on focusing on the Identified Patient and on themselves as parents of a sick or bad child, the prognosis for an early, successful outcome in therapy is not as good.

c. Also, if the child (the I. P.) helps the parents to keep the focus on himself (schizophrenics and delinquents do this), the therapist has the extra task of trying to reassure the I. P. that it is safe to talk about the pain between his parents, while at the same time reassuring the mates.

5. Family therapy is, in one sense, a form of marital therapy, even though the family therapist also deals with the mates in their parental roles.

a. But how the therapist deals with the parental role depends on the age of the children. As I see it, the parental role only exists in relation to children who are still in the family and not yet of age. After a child is twenty-one, he must be treated as another adult, because this is the reality he and his parents must be educated to accept if they have not yet been able to do so (see page 138).

b. Family therapy must be focused primarily on the mates as mates because their marital pain has prevented them from parenting their child according to his growth needs. They have parented him according to their needs.

c. Family therapy must be focused primarily on the mates as

mates because their marital pain is what the Identified Patient and all other children in the family are most acutely attuned to and affected by.
-- Parents who are unhappy with each other cannot give a child a feeling that his home base is secure.
-- Nor can they be helpful models for the child of what a comfortable, rewarding male-female relationship is like.

6. Once the therapist has briefly dealt with the problem as the family defines it, he then starts with the chronology, commencing with the mates. *

   a. The mates were around first; they are, in fact, the architects of the family.
      -- By dealing first with the mates, the therapist also starts to delineate the marital relationship.
      -- He also helps the child to see his parents as people who had lives long before he was born.
   b. He starts with the mates, even though the family, as a family, did not begin to exist until the arrival of the first child. If he started with each parent's relationship to his child, he would be putting the cart before the horse.

7. The nucleus of the later family group began to exist when the mates first laid eyes on each other and decided to continue the relationship.

   a. At this stage, the basic marital homeostasis (or definition of relationship) began to be formed. So any chronology must begin at this first meeting between the two future mates.
   b. The male and female who decided to continue the relationship may have spent some time forming one before they got married. So any chronology must cover the period between the first meeting and marriage.
   c. The male and female who became mates probably lived together for a while as a childless couple. So any chronology must cover the period before the mates took on the parental role.
   d. Also, both mates had, themselves, grown up in a family. So any chronology must include some picture of what life was like in both original family environments. (Although this information belongs chronologically first, the therapist must be present-family oriented, so he starts with the period when the mates first met each other; he starts with the beginning of the present family.)

---

*As he does this, the therapist may take notes, either to refresh his own memory, for research purposes, or to show the family that he takes their history seriously. On the other hand, many therapists will tape interviews or will find note-taking disruptive. This, since Freud's early remarks on the matter, remains an individual problem.

8. Before going into the actual questions the therapist can ask and the order in which he can ask them, let me emphasize the manner, spirit, or style in which the therapist must ask his questions.

   a. The family therapist takes the family life chronology in a casual yet attentive way (see page 163).
   b. He behaves as though he were a family chronicler, out collecting facts on family life. He does this in an atmosphere of hopeful discovery; the family and he together are going to paint a picture of the past. All members will have perceptions of events to offer, even though one person's perceptions may not jibe with those of another.
   c. He does not behave like a census taker, a funeral director, or a district attorney interrogating the accused. He and the family are scientists, working together on a task. For example, the therapist can say:

      "Then Grandma comes back into the picture. Is that right? When did that happen, as you remember it? Before or after Suzie, here, came on the scene?"

9. The therapist first gets what I call a Cast of Characters, as if he were orienting himself to a drama:

      "Well, now, to get a fuller picture of this, tell me who is in your family."

      "What are the names of your children? Where are they now? What are their ages?"

   It is wise to remember that there may be other children in the family besides those present in the therapy room.

10. If the therapist finds that one or both mates had previous marriages, he pauses to ask for names, ages, whereabouts of previous mate and children from previous marriages. He also asks for date of previous marriage, date of divorce from or death of previous mate.

      "I see. Then you have been married before. Then this is a family made up of some children from that previous marriage."

      "When did you first marry?"

      "What led to the separation?"

   Often the father in the therapy room is really a stepfather or an adoptive father. Such questions about the Cast of Characters quickly reveal possible problem areas in the present family.

11. The therapist finds out if any other people are presently living with the family, people such as in-laws. boarders, aunts, etc. He also asks about any persons <u>not</u> still in the family who have received or contributed nurture, financial support or direction (guidance-discipline) in the past.

> "Are there any other people living with you now?"

> "Are there any other persons who at any time in the past have been members of this family?"

> "When did each come into the family?"

> "What was the reason that each joined the family?"

> "Where did each come from?"

> "When did each leave the family?"

> "What was the reason for leaving the family?"

> "Where did each go?"

> "Where is each of these persons now?"

> "What is the contact between each of these persons and each of the present family members now?"

> "I see, then we have all the people who were or are part of this family."

By constantly repeating the idea of "this family," the therapist helps the family (especially the parents) to see that they are, in fact, a unique unit. Also, by checking on the whereabouts of all family members, the therapist may discover that a daughter is in a mental hospital nearby and one mate's parents live right around the corner. In other words, many people who are not in the therapy room may be very much in the picture. The therapist must know about them.

12. The therapist then defines the therapy task, giving his own orientation:

> "As you know, we work with families here. And we have found that when one member has pain, all share this pain in some way. Our task is to work out ways in which everyone can get more pleasure from family life. Because I am sure that at one time this family had better times."

By speaking in general, the therapist prevents any specific member from feeling responsible for the unhappiness in the family.

118

Also, by accentuating the idea of pleasure as the goal of therapy, the therapist continues to decrease fear and increase hope.

Finally, by talking about "what we see" in families, the therapist uses his special knowledge about families in order to help family members to see themselves as not especially bad or hopeless.

13. The therapist then shifts to the mates as the leaders of the family:

> "Well, now, you two haven't been parents all your lives. You knew each other long before 'this one' (the I. P.) came along. Tell me, how did you two happen to choose each other as mates?"

By shifting to an earlier period in order to approach the marital relationship, the therapist continues to decrease threat. The period he is asking about is when both mates felt more hopeful than at present. And, with follow-up questions, the therapist continues to expand information on earlier expectations:

> "What was it about her that led you to say, 'She's for me'?"

> "Well, there must have been other fellows at the dance, too. Why this one in particular?"

14. The therapist asks about steps taken to continue the relationship:

> "So when did you meet again? Who took that important next step? How did it come about?"

> "So he called you up. What did you do? Did you expect him to do this? What did you expect her to do?"

> "And then what happened?"

> "When did you both agree that you wanted to continue the relationship?"

> "When did you two announce to the world that you were serious about your courting?"

The two mates usually get quickly involved talking about this almost-forgotten time. And the child, left in the appropriate role of observer, has an opportunity to see his parents as two people who lived before he did and once had a happier relationship with each other.

Questions about this period also continue to delineate the mates as mates, and each mate as an individual who has made a decision to live with the other in marriage. The effect of these questions on the mates seems to be: "We <u>were</u> happy once. We can be again." The effect of these questions on the child seems to be: "My parents were <u>happy</u> once. Maybe they can be again."

15. The therapist turns to the child (or I. P.) repeatedly during this meeting-and-marriage story, and asks him if he knew about this period of his parents' lives:

> "Maybe it's hard to believe that at one time your parents didn't even know each other."

> "Did you know this about Dad? That he was struggling to earn enough money so he could marry your Mother?"

> "Did you know that your Mother thought so little of herself that she believed no man would want to marry her?"

Even if the child refuses to answer the therapist, these questions still continue. By speaking to the child in front of his parents (an "aside"), the therapist can begin to give interpretations not only to the child but indirectly to his parents. He starts communicating his view of their "worthwhileness" at the same time that he takes the chronology.

16. The therapist asks about the decision and plans for the marriage:

> "When did you decide to marry? How did you go about making plans to marry?"

> "What was the marriage ceremony like? Who was there?"

> "What obstacles stood between you and marriage?"

These questions bring out realistic details about income, war, job changes, death or illness of parents, etc. They also emphasize the idea that both mates chose each other; their marriage did not just happen.

The questions also bring out problems which either or both mates had in separating from, yet trying to please, their own parents. (For example, you often find out that the mates went through two marriage ceremonies in order to please their parents.)

These questions also give the I. P. a coherent story about the natural development of the family. This unraveling of the past helps undistort reality.

17. The therapist asks for each mate's idea of the other mate's response when the decision to marry came up:

"When was the idea of marriage first talked about? In what context? How was the idea communicated? What was said? Who first mentioned it?"

"What was your (husband's) picture of your wife's response?"

"What was your (wife's) picture then of your husband's response?"

"What were you (wife) thinking and feeling when your husband asked you to marry him? What did you (husband) feel?"

18. If there are discrepancies in the two pictures, the therapist tries to reveal and interpret them. He uses this instance to begin introducing the couple to the idea that they may be operating from an insufficient understanding of each other and that there are ways to correct such misunderstandings. He states:

"You (wife) were feeling and thinking something different from what your husband thought you were feeling and thinking. "

"How do you explain that your husband got a picture about what you were feeling and thinking that was different from what you actually were feeling and thinking?"

"How do you (husband) explain that you got a different picture from that which your wife was feeling and thinking and from what you intended?"

"Does this situation ever occur in the reverse, that is, that you (wife) get a different picture from what you (husband) intend?"

"What happens when either of you sees that each of you somehow has not gotten the other's message? This of course happens to everyone. Everyone needs techniques to handle this. "

"What happens when each of you turns up with different pictures of presumably the same thing?"

"What techniques do you know about that you (wife) and you (husband) have developed to handle this situation?"

"This could sometimes look as if someone were lying, or that they were bad, stupid, sick, or crazy. "

"I think this is an area where we need to do some work. Now let's get back!"

19. The therapist then asks about parental reactions to the decision to marry:

> "How did your parents react to your courting and decision to marry?"

> "Where were your parents living at the time? Where were you living at the time?"

These questions naturally lead to information about each mate's relationship with his or her own parents. Usually this area is emotionally loaded and also leads to early marital conflicts.

The therapist gears the chronology to the responses he receives from the family. If one or both mates show an interest in discussing their premarital lives, the therapist pauses in his chronology of events in the nuclear family and now concentrates on the chronology of each mate's life in his family of origin. Such a diversion further delineates each mate as an individual with a separate premarital life of his own.

20. The therapist then goes further into the relations between the engaged pair and their future in-laws. He directs the following series of questions to the wife and repeats them for the husband:

> "What did you (wife) know about how your father felt about your marrying your husband? How did you know this?"

> "What did you know about how your mother felt about your marrying your husband? How did you know this?"

> "What did you know about how your husband's mother felt about having you for a daughter-in-law? How did you come to know this?"

> "How did you know about how your husband's father felt about having you for a daughter-in-law?"

> "Did you (husband) have the same impression as your wife?" (If different, the therapist will label the fact that there is a difference and what the difference is.)

> "How do you account for the difference in your impressions?"

21. The therapist goes on to ask about the couple's present relations with their in-laws:

> "How are things now between you (wife) and your mother-in-law, your father-in-law, your mother, your father?"

"How are things now between you (husband) and your mother, your father, your father-in-law, your mother-in-law?"

"How would you like things to be different?"

22. The therapist now expands the Cast of Characters to include each mate's brothers, sisters, mother, father, aunt, etc.

"Both of you came from your own family environments. We'd better get a picture of who is in these families."

"Do you have brothers and sisters? How old are they? Younger or older than you?"

"Then that makes you the eldest in the family."

"What are their names? Where are they living now? Are they married? Do they have children? How old are their children?"

"Where are your parents living now? How old are they? What does your father do for a living?"

Because this area is usually loaded, the therapist first concentrates on facts: names, ages, sex, whereabouts of family members. In this way he gets a picture of what each mate's family environment must have been like. He puts off details about relationships and feelings until he has some loose framework to fit them in. He does not encourage a family member to wallow in feelings until he has some idea what the feelings may be about. He constantly relates feelings and perceptions to time, place and context.

These questions about each mate's pre-marital environment also give the therapist clues as to what people in the extended family, or family of origin, have been influential in the lives of the people in the nuclear family. These questions also show the present geographical spread and cluster of all these influential people.

23. After expanding the Cast of Characters to include the two families of origin, the therapist asks each mate to describe his two parents.

"If I were to meet your (husband's) mother in a railroad station, how would I recognize her? How would I know your father?"

"If I had the opportunity to talk to your (wife's) mother, what would she tell me about how food, money, sex, discussion of children and fun were handled in your family? What would your father tell me?"

By asking perceptual questions, the therapist can help each mate give information about his relationship to his parents without calling up anxiety. And the therapist can receive more clues on the models from which both mates are operating.

24. As he concentrates on each mate's relationship to his own parents, the therapist can introduce several new concepts into the family ideology, and introduce them in the least threatening way, since they are one step removed from the nuclear family. Here he introduces the concept that people are different. He says, to each mate in turn:

> "I noticed as you were talking that your mother and father were alike in these ways, and different in these ways." (And he labels the differences.)

> "How did you see them manage to live with these differences?"

25. Different-ness is a loaded idea in dysfunctional families. By reminding the mates that they were children once, observing their parents as different, the therapist begins to introduce the idea that their child sees them as different. That it is all right to be different. The therapist can say:

> "Everyone needs ways to handle the presence of differences. It looks as if in your (wife's) family it was handled like this. In your (husband's) family it was handled like this."

> "How do you (wife) see yourself as like your husband?"

> "How do you see yourself as different from your husband?"

> "How do you (husband) see yourself as like your wife?"

> "How do you see yourself as different from your wife?"

> "What ways have you each worked out to live with your differences from each other?"

> "How do these ways work out?"

26. The therapist concludes by pointing out the unsuitability of the husband's, or wife's, ways of handling different-ness:

> "It looks as if you both have been trying to use the same ways that your parents used."

> "Of course, you (wife) are like no one else and you (husband) are like no one else. All people are different. No one exactly duplicates anyone else."

"It looks as if the ways you are using fitted your parents all right, in their time and place, but they don't fit <u>you</u> — we need to find ways that fit you as you both are."

"Perhaps, without your knowing it, you (husband) have been behaving toward your wife as though she were your mother, and you (wife) have been behaving toward your husband as though he were your father."

"Perhaps, without knowing it, you (husband) have been expecting your wife to respond like your mother and have behaved toward her accordingly. And you (wife) may have expected your husband to respond to you like your father and so you behaved toward him accordingly."

<u>"Our parents are our first teachers. We get our ideas of how to behave from what we see, what we experience and what we are told, and all this comes to us from our first teachers. You got your ideas from your respective first teachers."</u>

27. The therapist introduces the idea that people disagree. He asks each mate:

"Of course everyone disagrees at times. Were your mother and father able to disagree openly?"

"How did you see your mother and father go about disagreeing?"

Both mates still suffer from varying degrees of prohibition against commenting on pain which they saw existing between their own parents. The therapist not only receives clues on the degree of the prohibition but also begins to relieve the mates from it.

28. The therapist introduces the idea that pain can be looked at and commented on (see page 169):

"Did you see your parents' pain?"

"Were you able to relieve their pain?"

"How did you go about it?"

"How did Mother respond when you tried to help?"

"How did Father respond when you tried to help?"

These questions continue to remind the mates that they were children once, observing their own parents. A dysfunctional parent has difficulty seeing the child as the child is. The therapist begins to stimulate this awareness by reminding the parent of how he felt as a child, by helping the parent to step, temporarily, back into the child's shoes. But he stimulates this awareness where it is safe, one step removed from the present nuclear family.

29. The therapist introduces the idea that people can have fun:

> "What did your parents do for fun?"

Dysfunctional people have as much trouble talking about pleasure as they have talking about pain.

30. The therapist, in eliciting information about each mate's pre-marital life, helps highlight discrepancies between what the parents did and what they told their children to do:

> "How did you (wife) see your mother treat your father?"
>
> "How did you see your mother treat you?"
>
> "How did your mother tell you to treat your father?"
>
> "How have you explained the difference?"

The therapist repeats these questions to the husband. These questions indirectly show the mates the kinds of questions their child may be asking of them.

31. The therapist, in eliciting information about each mate's pre-marital environment, shows that family events affect different members:

> "So your father lost his job just about the time you were hoping to go to college? How did the family cope with this problem?"

32. The therapist, in eliciting information from each mate, tries to weave back and forth between the mates in order to keep the information at the same time and developmental period:

> "Let's see, then, by the time you had managed to get yourself to college your wife, here, must have started high school. Let's find out how she got herself up to this period."

33. The therapist also compares one mate's experience with the other mate's experience:

> "Well, now, evidently you (husband) saw your father leave the house when he and your mother disagreed. What did

you (wife) see your father doing?"

"I gather that things in your (husband's) house seemed pained but quiet whereas in your (wife's) house people were fighting openly all the time. Am I right?"

34. Sometimes one mate's premarital story will be extensive and productive for therapy, so the therapist continues to concentrate on that mate. If so, he turns to the other mate and says:

"We'll have to get to you next time, I guess, and find out how things were going for you during this period."

In effect, the therapist says: "There is enough to go around. Everyone will have the chance to tell his story. Everyone will be included in therapy."

35. The therapist brings both mates' chronology up to the time of marriage. He then accentuates the idea that people are influenced by past models. And he asks for information on how the mates translated what they had learned:

"Well, now, we have some idea of each of your models. Let's see how these growing-up experiences influenced how you two went about being married."

First he asks the mates what plans for their future life were made at the time of their marriage, and what ideas they had about it:

"Where were you planning to live?"

"What were the plans for how the two of you would be supported?"

"What were the plans about how you were going to divide household tasks?"

"What were the plans for handling, distributing, and spending money?"

"What arrangements had you made for quarreling and disagreeing, which everyone who is close to somebody else is bound to do from time to time?

"What arrangements had each of you made for the individual interests of the other?"

"What plans had you made for having children?"

"When did you plan to have a child or children?"

"How many did you want?"

"What sex children had you hoped for?"

"What plans had you made for having fun?"

"What did each of you think about where you would be, what you would be doing, and what you would look like ten years after the marriage? Twenty years after the marriage?"

36. Then the therapist asks what actually did take place. For example, he will ask about the early days of the marriage:

"Did you have a honeymoon? Where? How long? How did it go?"

"Where did you set up housekeeping?"

"Were either of you continuing schooling after you married?"

"Were you working? Where?"

"You went into the Army at that time? When was that? Before or after your mother moved in to live with you and your wife?"

The therapist keeps track of each person in terms of age as he moves through time from the marriage date to the present. As each event comes along, he asks how it came to be, who first mentioned the idea, and under what circumstances. He finds out what the other thought and how he responded to the idea. He ascertains who came into the family, who left. The therapist uses these questions to create a sequential picture of the past, cross-referring all information. He also uses them to further delineate problem areas and success areas. Often such questions don't have to be asked; the mates will volunteer the answers.

37. The process of getting this information serves other therapy purposes too.

   a. By focusing on the mates when they were childless, the therapist further accentuates the idea that the mates have a relationship separate from the parental role.
   b. Also, by emphasizing the influence of the past, he continues to decrease blame and threat. He helps to make past and present behavior look more understandable.

38. The therapist asks each mate what he had expected from marriage:

"What did you want your marriage to be like?"

This question helps the therapist find out what distortions each mate would have to make in order to explain away disappointment. For example, was the wife looking primarily for a roof over her head? Or for someone to comfort her? Or for the ice cream she never had enough of as a child? Was the husband looking primarily for enough to eat? For uncritical devotion? For regularly darned socks?

39. The therapist checks out whether expectations, hopes, fears, got communicated:

> "Did you tell her this? That food was very important to you? Did she know that you always feared you might starve?"

> "Did you tell him that a house had a special meaning for you?"

40. The therapist asks what things each mate particularly liked in the other and whether each had (and has) a clear way of expressing these feelings. He asks this of the husband (and then puts the same series of questions to the wife):

> "What things do you remember that you found pleasant and and satisfying in your wife?"

> "Did you (wife) know that he thought these things about you?"

> "If you did, how did you come to find this out?"

> "If not, how do you (husband) explain that she did not know?"

> "Was it that you (wife) did not ask or that you (husband) did not tell?"

> "Do you (wife) know about his thoughts in regard to this now?"

41. The therapist brings up the concept of different-ness again, this time in a present-day context. He asks each mate what he did not like about the other mate and how he planned to deal with these disliked qualities. (The following questions are later redirected toward the other mate.)

> "What things do you remember finding out about each other that were unpleasant, new, different, or even bad? There are always imperfections in people and each is different from the other."

> "Did you (husband) know that your wife felt this about you?"

> "If yes, how did you find out?"

"If not, how did you (wife) explain that your husband did not know?"

"What ways did you (wife) have in mind about coping with what you saw was unpleasant (or 'different' or 'bad') in him?"

"How have these worked out?"

"Do you (husband) know what your wife's thoughts are in regard to this now?"

42. The therapist points up discrepancies and asks the mates to explain how they have integrated them. The wife's nagging seemed protective before marriage. Now it is seen as domineering. The husband's forgetfulness seemed lovable before marriage. Now it is seen as irresponsible. Each thought that love and time would conquer all.

"How have you explained it to yourself that some things you hoped for haven't worked out?"

"How have you explained it to yourself that you need to have enough to eat yet chose a wife who hates to cook?"

"How can it be that you need to feel secure by owning a house, yet you chose a husband who hates to stay in one place?"

These questions help the therapist find out how much the relationship was based on uncommunicated hopes rather than on communicated reality-testing. The therapists' comments, by highlighting the discrepancy between hopes and marital choice, also shows each mate that he had some responsibility for his marital choice.

43. The therapist explains discrepancies by referring to the models from each mate's past, and also by accentuating the need for clear communication:

"I guess something else was going on here that led you to think you could not ask for what you wanted. Maybe you felt you had to crawl under the carpet like your mother."

"I guess you thought you had to please the ladies all the time. That's what you saw your dad doing. Maybe that's why you couldn't ask for what you wanted."

These statements continue to relate the past to the present. But they also imply that the past need not continue to influence the present and that people can free themselves from this influence.

44. The therapist continues the chronology to include plans for and arrival of each child. He also explores the physical circumstances at the time of birth. He repeats his questions for each child, since each child is a different experience in parenting. Usually the mates had only the barest notion of how parenting would affect their lives, especially of how it would affect their relationship as mates.

> "When did you both decide to include parenting in your lives?"

> "Which sex child had you hoped for first?" (to each)

> "Where was this?"

> "How did the birth go?" (to wife)

> "Where were you?" (to husband)

> "When did each of you decide you wanted to become a parent?"

> "What do you suppose was the reason you wanted to become a parent at that particular time?" (to each)

> "How long did it take after your decision before conception took place?"

> "What do you suppose stood in the way?" (if it was a long period)

> What kinds of changes did you think would come about when the baby came?" (to each)

Here the therapist brings in a "universal truth": "Changes always come when a baby comes," to suggest that the couple is not unusual in finding a new baby a strain. Then:

> "How did you plan for these changes?" (to each)

> "How have these plans worked out?"

> "What kind of changes actually did come about for you?"

45. The therapist moves on to ask about the younger children, not forgetting that there may also be other children by an earlier marriage, now living elsewhere:

> "Do you have other children?" (to each)

> "Now let's see – when did you decide to have the next child?"

"Do you remember what you thought the first time you saw your first child? Your second child?" (to each)

"Do you remember what kind of an adult you hoped your child would be?" (to each)

"What kind of plans did you make for the care of the first child when the second child was making his entrance into the world?"

"How did that go?"

"Now, you have two children, a male of three, and an infant girl?"

"What were your observations about how the first child was welcoming the second child?" (to each)

"How had you prepared the first child for the coming of the second child?"

"At this point in time, which one of your children seems most like you?" (to each)

"Which one seems most different from you?" (to each)

"Is there anyone in either of your respective families that any child resembles more than yourself? Who is that person?"

The therapist, by these questions, continually cross-refers information which he has received in order to highlight the realistic concerns which new families have when taking on the parental role. In effect, he lets the parents know that he sees them as having other concerns besides parenting, and as having had to juggle many different kinds of life needs. He also receives clues about how each mate integrated what he expected from the child with what the other mate expected.

46. The therapist tries to get a picture of how much time the members of the family spend together:

"Let's see how a day goes in your house. Who first sees the light of the day?"

"Then who gets up next?"

"Who does that person see when he or she gets up?"

"Then who? Who does that person see? If the other per-

sons in the household already up are gone, where and
when did they go?"

The therapist goes on with this until everyone in the household is
up, then he takes them through the day to bedtime. Then he makes
a statement about the literal clock time that all have for face-to-
face contact. He asks about the means everyone has of letting the
others know what is going on in his life in the absence of
face-to-face contact. If there is no means, then he suggests
that each person has a concept of what the others are doing during their absence. He finds out what these concepts are, and
checks with the other persons to ascertain the accuracy of the
concepts.

47. The therapist will now try to get a picture of the home. He asks
who sleeps where? Who eats together? When is eating done? He
tries to get an idea of the atmosphere of the family's life together.
He may ask, for example: "If I were in your house during any
evening meal or breakfast, what would I see and hear?" (he asks
this of each family member, starting with the husband and wife,
then going on to the children, oldest first.)

48. The therapist now begins to echo the questions he has asked of
the parents by asking some of the same questions of their child
(and he accompanies his questions with encouraging and inter-
pretive statements):

"Do you see your parents as able to have fun? What do you
see them doing that is fun?"

"How do you see your parents as different? (Well, one thing
we know for sure: Dad is a male and Mother is a female.)"

"Do you see your parents as able to disagree openly? How
do you see them going about it?"

"Are you able to relieve their pain? How does Dad respond
when you try? How does Mother respond when you try?"

By this stage in the chronology, the therapist has (hopefully) built
a safe, understanding framework within which child and mates
will be able to comment on what they see and hear. But the therapist is still working against great odds with the child: the child is
responding to prohibitions against commenting or even against
asking questions.

The therapist continues to accentuate "pain" rather than "who did
what to whom?" He now overtly works at releasing the child from
parental prohibitions against comments. Also, by asking the child
to communicate his perceptions of his parents, the therapist helps
the parents receive another view of themselves. Children are very

protective of their parents. The more dysfunctional the family, the more protective the children will be. So whatever the children say will be said with great care. Often the parents react by saying, "I never knew that he was aware of all this!"

49. If the child has difficulty commenting, the therapist helps him to do so, and interprets for him:

> "Maybe you are afraid that you will hurt Mother and Dad if you let them know that you see their pain."

> "Maybe you think that if you simply report on what you see and hear, Mother and Dad will only have more pain."

> "I think you do see your parents' pain. But maybe you feel you cannot comment."

> "I'm sure Mother and Dad want to know what you see and hear. But maybe they think you don't want to tell them."

50. By this time, the interview is nearing an end. The therapist brings about closure and at the same time stimulates hope:

> "Well, it seems clear that everyone is trying to please everyone else, but no one seems to be successful at this. How can this be! We'll have to work on this!"

> "Once we get all the pieces together so that they make sense this kind of robbery won't have to go on any longer."

> "I have the feeling that we can come to some new ideas about all this."

> "We'll see what else we can learn about all of this. I have the impression that once all of these things get put in their right places, there won't be any more pain."

People do not dare go from the known to the unknown without hope, especially if they are operating within a fearful, critical environment.

51. The family life chronology, as outlined here, looks entirely too neat.

a. Interviews are, of course, never this structured or this orderly.
b. Nor does the therapist plow through a chronology regardless of the kind of responses he receives from the family.
c. After all, one of the main purposes of taking a chronology is to shift focus from the Identified Patient to the marital relationship in the least threatening way.

d. If the mates are so fearful that they resist such a shift, the therapist must change his order and change his emphasis slightly.

52. The chronology listed here is really a general plan from which the therapist deviates, depending on responses he receives to questions.

   a. Via this plan, he introduces new concepts into the family's ideology, concepts to which he will return in later sessions.
   b. Via this plan, he can move quickly but safely into his role as therapist, find out what he needs to work on first, what can wait.
      -- He behaves like a dentist who asks the patient, "Where is the pain?" and then proceeds to look where the patient points and explore further.
      -- He relies on the family to help him, but he never forgets that he is the leader of the therapy process.

MAIN FLOW OF FAMILY-LIFE CHRONOLOGY

TO FAMILY AS A WHOLE:

Therapist asks about the problem

TO MATES:

Asks about how they met, when they decided to marry, etc.

TO WIFE:	TO HUSBAND:
Asks how she saw her parents, her sibs, her family life.	Asks how he saw his parents, his sibs, his family life.
Brings chronology back to when she met her husband.	Brings chronology back to when he met his wife.
Asks about her expectations of marriage.	Asks about his expectations of marriage.

TO MATES:

Asks about early married life. Comments on influence of past.

TO MATES AS PARENTS:

Asks about their expectations of parenting. Comments on the influence of the past.

TO CHILD:

Asks about his views of his parents, how he sees them having fun, disagreeing, etc

TO FAMILY AS A WHOLE:

Reassures family that it is safe to comment.

Stresses need for clear communication.

Gives closure, points to next meeting, gives hope.

Chapter XIII

Including the Children in Family Therapy

1. Many therapists wonder how to introduce children into family therapy.

   a. Even a therapist who has had practice in seeing marital pairs together in therapy is often apprehensive about bringing children in too. It seems a difficult enough task to work with an unhappy marital pair, let alone with two generations at once.
   b. The presence of children might spell anarchy to the therapy process.
      -- Children, especially little ones, have limited attention spans and act impulsively.
      -- How can a verbal process like therapy hold their interest?
      -- How can a child be expected to sit still for an hour or more?

2. Even though the idea of family therapy seems to make sense to a therapist, he may still wonder what rules he should hold to.

   a. Should he include all the children who are in the family, even the little ones?
   b. Or should he limit therapy to the two parents and the child who happens to have symptoms.
   c. Should he include the children right from the beginning? If not, when should he bring them in?
   d. Once in, how long should the children stay in?
   e. Once in, what guidelines should the therapist follow in order to keep control of the therapy process?
   f. Does the presence of children turn family therapy into child therapy?

3. Let me try to explain how I have answered these questions for myself. I will also give a picture of how I, as therapist, proceed. Let us say that Johnny is the I. P. He has a sister, Patty, and a mother and father called Mary and Joe.

   a. Johnny, by his behavior, is sending "SOS" signals about family pain.
   b. As I have said before, I include Johnny in therapy with his par-

ents because I see his symptoms as a family phenomenon to be treated by a family approach.

4. What about the other children in the family, in this case, Patty? If Patty has no symptoms, do I still include her in therapy?

   a. Some family therapists do not include Patty unless she begins showing symptomatic behavior too.
   b. I do include Patty because Patty is still part of the family homeostasis even though she is not serving an I. P. function.
   c. I operate from the assumption that when there is pain in the family, all family members feel it in some way. Patty, too, is affected by the pain between her parents, and though she shows no symptoms now, she may later on.
   d. I believe that the family therapist can do a great deal of preventive work by including all the children in the therapy process.
     -- As the therapist works to help the family redefine its relationships, Patty can become very involved and may benefit as much as her brother does.
     -- And, because every family member has his own perceptions about what is going on in the family, Patty will have as much to contribute to the therapy process as her brother.

5. If Johnny and Patty are very young, is it still important to include them in therapy? After all, one might say that since the problem exists mainly between the marital pair, Patty and Johnny will benefit just as much if they stay home while their parents go in for some marital therapy. Besides, any problem that such children have is probably not "internalized" yet, so a change in the family environment should produce changes in the children even if they are not present at therapy sessions.

   a. It is true that Patty and Johnny will benefit if I see only their parents in marital therapy. That is why sometimes I do see the marital pair when the children are four or younger.
   b. But I still make it a point to bring all the children into therapy for at least two sessions so that I can see with my own eyes how the family, as a whole, operates.

6. I usually see the marital pair first, for at least two sessions. I do this because I consider it appropriate to start off family therapy with the marital pair.

   a. By asking to see the parents first, I say, in effect: "I see you two as the authorized leaders of this family. I also see you, apart from the children, as mates."
     -- In dysfunctional families, the mates have usually despaired of or abandoned their marital roles and have become just parents, focused on their children because they dare not focus on one another.
     -- By the time such a pair comes to me for help for their child,

very little of what I call "selfing" and of what I call "hus-
banding" and "wifing" is evident in their behavior. "Mothering" and "fathering" predominate in one form or another.
-- It seems appropriate, therefore, to begin with marital instead of family therapy, in order to remind the pair that
they are individuals as well as mates, mates as well as
parents.

b. If a family is so dysfunctional, however, that the mates cannot
bear to look at their own relationship but must have the child
there to focus on, I find it best not to begin with marital therapy
but to include the children right from the start. Though I do not
consider it appropriate, it is an exception I sometimes have
to make.

c. The age of the child helps to determine whether I include him
from the beginning or bring him in later. For instance, I include from the start an I. P. "child" who is over 21.
-- Many cases of schizophrenia are of this type.
-- Though the parents still regard the I. P. as a child, that in
itself is part of the family pathology and I do not want to reinforce it.
-- Therapists must always stand for reality. I make a point of
seeing this "child" and his parents together right away, because I know that the child's symptoms have a family function.
-- I make it clear that I am seeing three adults who are on an
equal plane with each other. I, by my behavior, am saying:
"I do not see your mother and father as still in charge of
you. Your mother, father, and I will not meet privately
first to decide what to do about you. "

7. How long do children stay in family therapy, once I bring them
in?

a. As I noted earlier, where the children are under four, I bring
them into therapy for at least two of the initial sessions. Otherwise, I work with the marital pair. Later on, though, I may
ask to have the I. P. included again in order to consolidate with
the child what the mates have learned from their marital therapy.

b. If the children are four or older, they will stay in family therapy for most of the sessions. However, I usually ask for a few
sessions along the way with just the marital partners, or with
other groupings or individuals (see pages 167-168):

c. Children who are over 21 are also likely to stay in family therapy for most of the sessions.
-- My aim is, of course, to bring such a "child" and his parents together so that I can eventually help separate them.
-- Unfortunately, it almost always takes many family therapy
sessions to achieve this goal.
-- In such a family, the child is never supposed to become an
adult.

8. Now let me describe how I proceed as therapist, once children have been included in the therapy process.

   a. First of all, during the marital therapy sessions, I try to prepare the parents for bringing the children in.
      -- Young parents especially are apt to be apprehensive. They wonder how their children will behave. They wonder what I will think of them as parents.
      -- I try to reassure them by commenting that of course seven-year-olds act like seven-year-olds, so why should their children be any different?
   b. Often I ask the parents how they plan to tell their children about the coming family therapy sessions.
      -- Mary may plan to say, "We are going to see a lady and talk about the family."
      -- Joe may plan to say, "We are all going for a ride in the car."
      -- This very question about how Mary and Joe communicate plans to their children can prepare the ground for later exploration into how clearly or unclearly they get their messages across in the family.
      -- In our marital therapy sessions, I have already introduced the idea that Mary and Joe are not very good at communicating with each other, so they will be prepared when I apply this concept to their parenting.

9. Now the day arrives for the first interview with the whole family. Let us say it is going to be an interview with very young children. How does the therapist control them? How does he keep them from bringing anarchy to the therapy process? I will try to make this point clearer in a minute by describing actual interview situations. For the moment, I will try to generalize my main therapy approach.

   a. I have found that a therapist has very few problems of control if he actively takes charge of the therapy process. If he knows how to do this, children respond as readily as their parents.
   b. There are, of course, some control problems.
      -- Patty wants to bang on the radiator. Johnny wants to keep going to the bathroom or the drinking fountain.
      -- Both constantly interrupt their parents, the therapist and each other in a mad dash to monopolize the airwaves.
   c. My general policy is, of course, to wait for the parents to do the controlling.
      -- The mother and father are the ones who should answer requests and set limits to their children's behavior.
      -- As a matter of fact, if I took over this role I would lose the very opportunity I am after, the opportunity to observe how the mother and father perform their parenting function.
   d. I do make it my responsibility, however, to communicate clearly the rules of behavior that apply in my own bailiwick,

the therapy room
-- No one may hit or play with the microphone or the recording
equipment, for example.
-- No one may destroy any chairs, window blinds, tablecloths,
etc.
-- No one (including parents, for that matter) may speak for
others.
-- Everyone must speak so he can be heard.
-- Everyone must make it possible for others to be heard.
"You are hurting my eardrums," I will say, or "You will
have to take turns talking or I can't do my work."
-- The parents will often ask me to set a rule about leaving
the therapy room. Mother will ask, "Is it all right if he
leaves?" I will say, "Yes," and then instruct the child on
how to find the water fountain or the toilet.
-- I also set rules on how often a child may leave the therapy
room. Usually one trip to the toilet and one trip to the water
fountain will give Johnny or Patty all the chance they need
to explore.
-- I also shorten the length of the therapy session to conform
to the ages of the children.
e. But, as I have already suggested, there is very little need for
control if the therapist conveys clearly, right from the beginning, that he is going some place. The children can get caught
up in the therapy process; they can become as engrossed in it
as their parents.

10. For instance, there are certain things I want to do from the beginning of family therapy. I want to use the opening sessions for
diagnosis, but I also want to use them for therapy. Therefore, I
try right away to introduce certain concepts that are usually foreign to the dysfunctional family. These concepts are probably fa-
miliar to you by now, but I think they can bear repeating. I want
the family members:

a. To recognize that they are individuals and are different from
one another.
-- Some are males, some are females. Some have red hair,
some brown. Some like roast beef, some hate it. Some
are young, some older.
-- Dysfunctional families have great trouble acknowledging
different-ness or individuality. In such families, to be different is to be bad and invites being unloved.
b. To recognize that they also have disagreements.
-- Some see a certain picture as beautiful, others see it as
ugly. Some think a certain piece of behavior is desirable,
others see it as undesirable.
-- Dysfunctional families often try to overlook or to "blur"
their disagreements, whether these are disagreements
over perception or over opinion.
c. To communicate with one another more clearly; to say what

they see, think, feel; to bring disagreements out into the open.
-- I especially want mates to see where they have been giving
conflicting messages to their children as well as to each
other. Marital communication sets the standard for parental
communication and for all communication between family
members.
-- I also want children and parents to be able to recognize and
comment on the pain existing between the marital partners.
-- I also want to help family members to communicate about
the behavior which brings them pleasure. As I have said,
· dysfunctional families have just as much trouble communicating about pleasure as they have communicating about
pain.

11. Here is a rather skeletal picture of a first interview with children present, pointing up the main emphases.

   a. To cover the points listed might take one interview with highly
   verbal young children, or it might take two or more.
   b. If even this summary seems long in reading, that is because
   it is described in slow motion here.
   c. However long it takes me to achieve my first therapy aims, I
   ask my questions in a warm, specific, matter-of-fact way.
   -- I ask many questions, believing that questions are in themselves therapeutic. This may be the first time that the children have been treated as people with perceptions and opinions.
   -- And, while I mostly concentrate on the children in the first
   family interview, I am indirectly speaking to the parents,
   too.

12. How the therapist can integrate children into family therapy:

   a. The therapist introduces the idea of individuality.
   -- He greets each child separately, calling him by name.
   -- He differentiates each child according to birth order and sex:

       "Let's see now. You are John. You are the eldest in the
       family."

   -- He repeats what each child says, to show that he is listening
   to the child:

       Th: How old are you, Patty?

       D: Seven.

       Th: You are seven.

   -- He asks questions over and over (especially with younger
   children) to say: "I am really talking to you." Often children will say they don't know or don't remember or give no

answer at all. But they will give the therapist clues to their answer in what they do. He does not leave an unanswered question without some closure. He says:

> "I see you are not ready to tell yet. We will come back to you later. I noticed you were looking at Mother and had a frown on your face. Maybe you are worried about what Mother will say."

-- He honors all questions from children to show that questions are not troublemaking and illegitimate, that people can ask questions about what they don't know.

> D: (whispering to Johnny) How old is Daddy?
>
> M: And I told him he could play outside if...
>
> Th: Excuse me just a minute. Patty had a question here, I think. You were wondering how old Dad is? Well Dad can tell you. It's all right to ask. If Dad doesn't want to tell you he can say so. How about it, Dad? Do you want Patty to know.

-- He assumes that children do hear, are interested, and are able to understand. They are not little-and-therefore-bad. He verbalizes his expectations so that children will rise to meet them.

> M: He isn't listening. He's always like that.
>
> Th: I'm not so sure. This fellow has his head screwed on right. He knows what's going on. But let's check with him.

b. The therapist introduces the idea of communication:
   -- He asks each child (according to birth order) what ideas he has about why he is here. (Little children feel pushed around.)

> Th: (to Johnny) What ideas did you have about where you were going today?
>
> S: I don't know.
>
> Th: Well you must have had some ideas about it. What did Mother tell you? What did Dad say? You must have figured out something to yourself.

-- He repeats what each child says (with clarifying interpretation) and goes on to the next child. (But not until he has some kind of answer from each child.)

Th: (to Patty) You thought you were going to talk? What did you think you were going to talk about?

D: Oh, the family.

Th: You got the idea that we were going to talk about the family. And Johnny, what ideas did you have?

-- He summarizes answers received from the children in terms of how clear they seemed to be about why they are in the therapy room:

"So Johnny thought he was going for a ride. Patty thought she was going to talk about the family. So you both had ideas about it."

-- He asks each child where he got his ideas about why he is here. Who told him? What was said?

D: Mother said we were going to talk about family problems.

Th: What about Dad? Did he tell you the same thing?

D: No.

Th: What did Dad say?

D: He said we were going for a ride.

Th: I see. So you got some information from Mother and some information from Dad. What about you, Johnny? Where did you get your information?

S: I don't remember.

Th: You don't remember who told you?

M: I don't think I said anything to him, come to think of it. He wasn't around at the time, I guess.

Th: How about you, Dad? Did you say anything to Johnny?

F: No, I thought Mary had told him.

Th: (to Johnny) Well,then, how <u>could</u> you remember if nothing was said?

S: Patty said we were going to see a lady about the family.

Th: I see. So you got your information from your sister, whereas Patty got a clear message from both Mother and Dad.

-- He asks how they handled differences in messages from their parents:

S: Daddy told Patty we were going for a ride.

Th: And Mother told Patty you were going to talk to a lady about the family?

S: Yeh.

Th: So what did you do with that? Dad is saying one thing and Mother another? You have to figure that one out. What did you make of that?

S: I figured we would go for a ride. And, uh, we would see a lady or something...

Th: I see. You decided that you would be doing both. So in this case, you were able to fit these things together -- what Mother and Dad said to Patty.

S: Uh huh.

-- He asks the mother and father what they remember saying:

Th: How about that, Mother? Were you and Dad able to work this out together -- what you would tell the children?

M: Well, you know, I think this is one of our problems. He does one thing with them and I do another.

F: I think this is a pretty unimportant thing to worry about.

Th: Of course it is, in one sense. But then we can use it, you know, to see how messages get across in the family.

-- He makes a general statement about communication:

"One of the things we work on in families is how family members communicate -- how clearly they get their messages across. We will have to see how Mother and Dad can get together so that Johnny and Patty can get a clear message."

c. The therapist briefly introduces the idea that family members
   can acknowledge parents' pain.
   -- He explains to the children why their mother and father
      have been coming here:

> "Well, now, I'll tell you why Mother and Dad have come
> here. They have come here because they were unhappy
> about how things were going in the family and they want
> to work out ways so that everyone can get more pleasure
> from family life. "

   -- He asks each child if he noticed that his mother and father
      were unhappy and asks for the evidence he uses for this
      perception:

> Th: Had you noticed that Mother and Dad weren't happy,
>   Patty?
>
> D: Yes, a little bit.
>
> Th: Well, I would think you could see when Mother and
>   Dad had pain. What have you noticed about this?
>
> D: Mother cries sometimes.
>
> Th: Mother cries sometimes. And, of course, tears
>   mean that Mother is feeling pain.
>
> D: Mother doesn't cry very often, though.
>
> Th: Of course Mother has her happy times, too. How
>   about Dad. Have you noticed when Dad has pain?

   -- He summarizes what each child has said and leaves the
      topic for the moment:

> "So Patty knows crystal-clearly when Mother has pain
> but she isn't quite as sure about Dad. Johnny says he
> hasn't noticed any pain except when Dad gets mad at him.
> We will find out more about that later. "

d. The therapist returns to the idea that family members can
   acknowledge different-ness, especially sex differentness,
   while at the same time he continues to establish rapport with
   each child.

   -- He asks each child in more detail about himself:

> Th: All right, we know Johnny is the eldest. He is also
>   the only boy. What grade are you in, Johnny?

S: Sixth.

Th: What do you like about school?

S: Baseball. I'm on first base.

Th: So we have a baseball player in the family. How about Dad, does he play baseball too?

S: Oh he's all right...

F: I used to play a little.

Th: So you both have this in common. What else do you like about school?

-- He makes general comments to each child about age problems each would be likely to have in relation to the other sib:

"Does this one get in your hair sometimes?"

"Does that one kind of push you around sometimes?"

"I would expect ten-year-old boys not to want little girls around."

-- He highlights the sex balance in the family:

" Then this is a family which has two females in it and two males in it. So nobody can be outnumbered in this family!"

"So you and Dad kind of hold up the male end of the household."

-- He asks each parent to describe each child in order to help them acknowledge different-ness:

M: Well, she is much quieter than he is. She tends to be more serious.

Th: You see Patty as the quiet one and the serious one. How about you, Dad? Is that what you see as different about the two?

F: Yes, she is more like her mother. Johnny isn't really like anyone in the family.

Th: Johnny seems so different that he doesn't seem like a member of the family?

F: Most of the time, the way he behaves, yes.

-- He helps children acknowledge ordinary different-ness between their parents:

> Th: How do you see your mother and your father as different, Johnny?
>
> S: I don't know.
>
> Th: Well, they have to be different, you know. No two people are alike. One thing we know for sure, Dad is a male, Mother is a female. That's a big difference.

e. The therapist introduces the idea that parents can have differences of opinion and disagreements, and can feel anger toward their children.
   -- He asks each child how he knows when Dad is angry:

> Th: (to Johnny) How does Dad go about showing his anger?
>
> S: He just gets mad.
>
> Th: Of course he does. Everybody gets mad sometimes. I would hope that Dad would have ways to let you know when he is not pleased with something you do. How does he show that he is mad?

-- He asks the same question about Mother:

> Th: How do you know, Patty, when Mother is angry with you?
>
> D: Oh, I know.
>
> Th: Then Mother is able to let you know this clearly?
>
> D: She spanks me.
>
> Th: She spanks you. Can you tell ahead of time when Mother will spank you?
>
> D: When I do something bad.
>
> Th: Like what?
>
> D: If I break my doll. If I go into the street...

-- He compares the two parents' ways of showing anger:

"Oh, so Dad shuts up and won't talk to you? You know
something is going on but maybe you aren't sure what.
Mother tells you right out what she doesn't like. Are
you sure what Dad is angry about? You seem to know
what displeases Mother."

-- He asks what things make each parent angry:

> Th: What do you know, as sure as tomorrow is Wednes-
> day, will make Dad blow his cork?

> S: If I play with his tools.

> Th: If you play with his tools. What else?

-- He asks how each child decides what to do if his parents
don't agree on what should be done:

> Th: Mother says you must play in your room. Dad tells
> you to play outside. Those are two different things.
> How do you know what to do?

> S: Uh...I...uh.

> Th: How can you know what to do?

> M: He plays both ends against the middle. That's what
> he does.

> Th: Well, of course he would have a problem here.
> Maybe if he does what Dad wants, then it looks as
> if he doesn't love Mother. He would have a prob-
> lem here as to what he should do.

f. The therapist introduces the idea that parents can have differences of opinion and can feel anger toward each other.
-- He asks each child how his parents go about disagreeing:

> Th: Of course everybody disagrees every once in a
> while. Let's see now, if I were in your house and
> Mother and Dad were mad at each other, what would
> I see?

> S: Mother goes to her room.

> D: Mother cries.

> Th: Mother would be in her room crying. And where
> would Dad be?

> S: Daddy usually beats it.

Th: Dad tries to solve things by leaving the house?

D: Daddy gets mad when Mother cries.

Th: How do you decide this? That Dad is mad because Mother cries?

D: He slams the door.

Th: I see. Dad slams the door. Mother is crying in her room. What do you see happening, Johnny?

-- He asks each mate to say how he or she knows when the other is angry or displeased:

Th: How about that, Dad? Do tears make you angry? Or are you already mad at Mary for something and then Mary cries?

F: Somehow... I don't know... somehow she has this way of letting me feel that it's me... that I am the one who...

Th: Mary's tears make you feel you've been the one who is wrong, is that it? You feel at fault?

F: Exactly. She won't listen when I try to explain.

Th: What about you, Mary? How do you know when Joe is displeased?

M: He turns on the TV so loud you can hear it in the laundry room.

Th: So then he shows his anger by shutting you out, is that it? And she shows her anger by shutting you out with her tears. And either way you can't find a way to get close enough to work things out.

-- He asks each mate what he does when other mate is angry, and how he tries to solve the disagreement:

F: I give in. That's what I do.

M: That's what you think. You're as stubborn as they come.

F: How? How am I more stubborn than you?

M: Many's the time I've come around to you.

Th: I think that...

S: Daddy, when are we going to the beach? You prom-
ised we could go, and we never do.

F: As soon as it's warmer we'll go. It's too cold to go
to the beach.

M: Of course we did promise them...

Th: I think we should...

D: You said we could go a couple of weeks ago.

Th: I think both children get upset when their mother and
father disagree. Maybe they think someone will get
hurt. But I don't see any dead bodies around, do you?
Mother looks in one piece. Dad looks in one piece.

M: They do get upset. We try not to argue in front of
the kids.

Th: But of course they know when their parents have
pain. The important thing is that ways can be found
to work on this. That's why we are here, to find
ways to work on this.

g. The therapist ends the first interview by introducing the idea
that each family member must show it when he is pleased by
what any of the others do.
   -- He asks each child what he can do that makes his mother
   or his father pleased.
   -- He asks each parent what he or she can do that pleases
   each child.
   -- He asks each mate what he can do that pleases the other
   mate.
   -- He comments on the information received:

   "Well, then, it seems everyone is clear on how to get
   everyone else's goat, but they are not clear on how to
   please each other. This is terrible. We'll have to work
   on this!"

13. So much for a skeletal picture of the first family interview with
young children. Now let us drop in at different times in later
family interviews to see what is going on. What is the family
therapist now doing? What is the family doing?

a. The therapist is still working to untangle the dysfunctional relationships which exist in unhappy families and which come
about primarily because the marital relationship is askew.

    -- Parents are abdicating from parenting.
    -- Parents are acting as sibs with their children, vying for attention from the other mate.
    -- Children are "parenting" their parents.
    -- Children are acting as ersatz mates of their parents.
    -- Children are successfully challenging appropriate parental authority.

b. Whatever family members are doing, the family homeostasis is precarious and all family members are feeling disappointed and puzzled.
    -- Nothing seems to turn out right.
    -- There never seems to be enough of anything to go around.
    -- Any relationship between any two members in the family makes the others feel left out.
    -- Evil motives are attributed to everyone.
    -- Everyone is feeling cheated.

c. Yet in spite of these conditions, the family as a whole still resists the efforts of any family member to change the family's way of operating. It takes a lot of therapist intervention to bring any pleasure to the family's life.

14. How the therapist can make parental behavior and child behavior understandable to family members.

a. The therapist helps parents to understand their children and receive "feedback" from them.
    -- He asks the parents to explain the child's behavior, thus making covert explanations overt so they can be dealt with. He challenges any solely negative interpretations and answers covert questions parents are asking about their children.

> M: His pleasure is doing things he knows will get me up in the air. Every minute he's in the house... constantly.
>
> Th: There's no pleasure to that, my dear.
>
> M: Well, there is to him.
>
> Th: No. You can't see his thoughts. You can't get inside his skin. All you can talk about is what you see and hear. You can say it _looks_ as though it's for pleasure.
>
> M: All right. Well, it looks as though, and that's just what it looks like constantly.
>
> Th: He could be trying to keep your attention, you know. It is very important to Johnny what Mother thinks.

-- He asks the child to explain his own behavior:

> F: I mean, he never wanted me to stay and watch him play baseball.
>
> Th: Tell me, how did you explain this to yourself? Why did you think he didn't want you to watch?
>
> F: Well, that's the trouble, I never have been able to figure it out.
>
> Th: Well, one way to find out is to ask. Let's ask Johnny. He can tell you. Maybe he is uneasy when Dad is around.
>
> S: I'd just get embarrassed, sometimes.
>
> Th: You'd get embarrassed.
>
> S: Uh huh. Cause he had Patty with him and Patty is always making a fuss. The other guys would laugh...

-- He helps the child to express frustration and anger and delineate situations which precipitate anger:

> Th: Do you kind of get mad at Daddy when he gets mad at you?
>
> S: Yeah, and sometimes he gets real mad and pinches my ear.
>
> Th: He pinches your ear. Do you feel like hitting him back?
>
> S: Yeah. I get real mad sometimes.
>
> Th: So what keeps you from hitting him?
>
> S: Well he's, uh, he's bigger than me.

b. The therapist helps children to understand their parents and to understand themselves as children.
-- He asks children to explain a parent's behavior, in order to challenge solely negative interpretations and add other possible interpretations:

> Th: Johnny, why do you think your mother wants you to eat?
>
> S: I don't know. She's always forcing things on me to eat.

Th: You know what? Let me tell you something about mothers. Mothers rack their brains trying to figure out what will please the family. Then, at the table, when you turn up your nose and say "That! I won't eat it!" what's mother to do? You are saying to her, "Take your food and stick it. I don't like it." Well, then mother feels, "What can I do? I don't know how to please you. OK, I won't try anymore. I can't please you, so I might as well not try."

-- He asks parents to explain their own behavior toward children:

Th: Tell me, why don't you want him to eat sweets?

M: I don't mind if he eats sweets, but he can't live on a constant diet of sweets.

Th: Well, why not? I thought everybody lived on a constant diet of sweets. Isn't that sensible?

M: No, and especially at that age. Your face breaks out and everything else.

Th: Why don't you let him be pimply? What do you care? What do you care like that for?

M: Well, I don't know...

Th: Well, see, I think...

M: All he does... he sleeps at our house and eats when he pleases, and that's about it.

Th: Do you hear in your mother's voice the irritation that she has when she's talking?

S: Yeah.

Th: Do you also have the feeling that this is a kind of desperation. She's thinking, "How am I going to get this guy grown up? He's going to grow up toothless and pimply and weak, and I can't do anything about it" (parents laugh)

-- He helps the child to express openly, and the parents to answer, covert questions the child is asking:

Th: (to Roger) You're not really sure yet why Dad adopted you, are you?

S: Uuuh.

Th: What?

S: I haven't been thinking about it.

Th: I think you should, because I think part of what you're thinking is that he only did it because your mother made him do it.

S: She can't make him do anything.

Th: Of course not! But then, you know, why did he do it then?

S: I don't know.

Th: Well, you've got to find some explanation, because your dad's a pretty sensible guy and he doesn't go around...

S: He must know why he did it.

Th: He must know?

S: Yes.

Th: Well, let's ask him. (pause) Sure he knows why he did it, but I wonder if you know.

S: I don't.

Th: (to father) Tell him again. Why did you adopt this bloke over here?

c. The therapist supports parental authority, at the same time recognizing that children are increasingly able to make good judgements and decisions for themselves.
-- He assumes that parents have the right and responsibility to "parent" their children:

> "You are the mother. You know what bedtime is best for seven-year-olds."

-- He assumes that children can take responsibility for what they do:

> Th: It was clear to you about when you were to be home, Johnny. What kept you from being home at that time?
> * * * * * * *
> D: I didn't <u>mean</u> to kick him.
>
> Th: Well, let's see now, Patty. It was your leg that some-

how landed against his leg. How can a leg do that all
by itself? That's very curious.

-- He checks out family rules:

Th: What is the rule in this family about watching television.

M: They can watch certain programs each night, up to
about nine.

Th: So you have definite rules about that?

M: Oh yes.

Th: What are some of the rules? Johnny, you tell me
what rules you know about.

M: Don't eat in the dining room. Don't leave clothes
around. Don't let the dog in the house

Th: These rules are very clear to you then? What was the
one about not eating in the dining room? That sounds
sort of strange to me.

M: Well, you see, we eat in the kitchen usually...

F: We use the dining room for guests.

Th: I see. So this family has a very special room
for when visitors come in.

-- He checks out family rule reinforcement:

Th: How does it go in the family, with discipline?

F: Oh, I don't know, I, ah...

M: We try to carry through when we make a promise.

F: Uh...

Th: Both ways?

F: Uh huh.

M: Good or bad.

F: Good or bad. Yes.

Th: Do you find yourself a little reluctant on that once
in a while?

M: No.

F: I, ah, try to keep it up, ah, if I tell him that he's not going to watch television... Of course, he does, he just, ah, that's another one. I told him for two weeks he can't watch television; first thing he's out there watching television.

d. He shows how marital disagreements produce difficulties in parenting (see example on pages 43-44).

e. The therapist helps mates restructure family relationships around a well-delineated marital relationship.
-- He helps parents separate themselves from their own parents:

Th: Were you the kind of a gal that could say to your mother: "Now Mama, I'm grown up now. No more of this"?

M: No, no, I won't talk back to my mother.

Th: Is that talking back, or is that stating a simple fact?

M: No, I couldn't conceive of it. Mother would get very mad.

Th: I think this has been a problem in this family.

F: Yes. Too much of one.

-- He helps mates to strengthen the marital relationship:

Th: What would you like to do?

M: Aaah, spend more time with him. I, I'm satisfied when he comes home; we don't have to particularly talk... I just like to be with him.

F: We like to camp.

M: And we like to camp.

Th: It's kind of natural, you know.

M: Yah! (sharp laugh)

Th: But you say it in a way that says you feel sad about it not happening more often.

M: I do! (long silence)

Th: Well, maybe that is an area where everyone can grow a little bit so that you can have more opportunity.

-- He helps equalize the parental responsibilities:

Th: Do you find it's easier to get your messages across to the kids when you and Dad are both home?

M: Yes.

Th: Have you any idea why that might be so?

M: Well, mmm, I don't know. Maybe he figures that Daddy's going to see that it stops -- whatever is happening...

Th: Does it cross your mind that it must be awfully tough for a woman to take the total responsibility for a family? Any woman would very much feel the loss of a husband during the week.

-- He helps strengthen same-sex parent-child relationships:

Th: (to Johnny) You mean you're making some shelves?

S: Yeh.

Th: You're making them with Dad?

S: No, I was watching one day. And we do a lot of Scout work together, and we made this little mail box.

Th: Good for you and Dad, that you have these times together.

-- He indirectly encourages same-sex parent-child relationships by questioning overdeveloped opposite-sex relationships:

Th: So you mean it's known in the family that you and Patty have always been quite close?

F: Real close, very close.

Th: (to mother) What about your son? Does he have the same kind of relationship to you?

F: Yes, oh yes.

M: (faintly) Yes, that's right.

Th: Is that how it is? A mother and son and daddy and daughter kind of thing?

-- He helps mates attend to each other more and to the children less:

Th: You know, both of you are turning yourselves inside out so much for your kids you have no time for yourselves.

M: I don't think we do more than parents should do.

Th: Well, tell me something. What are the two of you likely to do together?

S: I just had poison oak.

Th: What's that?

S: I just had poison oak a little while ago.

F: One of the hazards of camping.

M: Yes indeed.

S: I just had it the last time camping.

M: He lost two days of school that last week.

Th: And you went camping all that time?

S: Uh huh.

Th: What are you two likely to do if you just go off for a holiday or when you have time together?

M: He and I?

Th: Just you and George, yes.

M: We don't go off by ourselves as a rule.

F: We did once I think, aah, you know the last time we went down South we went to...

M: Oh, well, well, we had to, aaah...

F: We went to a funeral.

15. Theoretically, seeing families together in therapy makes good sense to most therapists, but they still feel apprehensive as to how to go about it. I hope this necessarily sketchy and incomplete description will give some idea of how it can be done.

   a. One fact we cannot overlook is that family therapy seems to make sense to the family itself.
   b. Husbands, in particular, participate readily in this kind of therapy.
   c. Both husband and wife repeatedly say, "We should have done this a long time ago."

Chapter XIV

Role and Technique of the Therapist

1. The therapist must first create a setting in which people can, perhaps for the first time, take the risk of looking clearly and objectively at themselves and their actions.

   a. He must concentrate on giving them confidence, reducing their fears, and making them comfortable and hopeful about the therapy process.
   b. He must show that he has direction, that he is going somewhere. His patients come to him because he is an expert, so he must accept the label and be comfortable in his role.
   c. Above all, he must show patients that he can structure his questions in order to find out what both he and they need to know.

2. The patient is afraid. He doesn't dare ask about what he doesn't know; he feels little, alone and frightened.

   a. He suffers from the Crystal Ball Syndrome: "I'm supposed to know. But I am little and can't ask. Yet I am big and omniscient; I can guess. You, the therapist, should be able to guess too."
   b. He suffers from the Fragility Syndrome: "If I ask, the other person will fall apart. If I ask, I will get an answer that will make me fall apart."
   c. He suffers from Fear of the Unknown. Pieces of the past are missing or can't be looked at. This or that is forbidden territory.
   d. He doesn't know what it is he doesn't know; he feels hopeless. He has been operating from insufficient information for a long time. He feels that there is no point in continuing the struggle.
   e. He can't ask about what he doesn't know; he feels helpless. Sick people can't be direct about what they want. They can tell about what hurts, not about what is wrong.
   f. He fears the therapist will lie to him; he feels suspicious. He assumes that others know and won't tell; that others see and hear everything. ("Ma always knew when I was in the cookie jar. So others know what is inside of me.")

3. The therapist is not afraid.

   a. He does dare to ask questions, and the way he frames them helps the patient to be less afraid as well.
      -- The therapist asks what the patient can answer, so that the patient feels competent and productive.
      -- The therapist engages the patient in a history-taking procedure to bring out details of family life. This makes the patient feel he knows things the therapist doesn't know, that he has something to contribute. (Patients get very involved in building this factual history of their own past. They argue with each other about the facts, correct the therapist, and so forth.)
      -- The therapist asks questions which the patient can emotionally handle at the time, so the patient can feel he is in control.
   b. The therapist doesn't know what it is he doesn't know, but he knows how to find out and how to check on his knowledge.
      -- The therapist does not assume anything. He must not think he knows more than he does. All he can assume is that there is a body before him; it is breathing; it is a male or a female of a certain age.
      -- If the therapist operates from assumptions without checking on them, he is often wrong. He must question his patients constantly:

        "Does she like being beaten, or not?"

        "Did they ever get to the movies?"

        "What does 'Well, sort of' mean?"

      -- He must question his own assumptions too. Does their coming late to the appointment mean they are "resisting" or not? (There is a story about a man accused by the therapist of "resisting" therapy because he arrived late for the therapy hour. Later the therapist discovered the man had been held up by a serious accident on the freeway.)
   c. The therapist can ask about what he doesn't know; he knows how to get facts.
      -- Facts about planning processes: "Did you get to the movies as you planned?" or, "Did you ever get the bread on the table?"

      -- Facts which reveal loopholes in planning. For instance, the mother complains that her children don't do chores. The therapist finds by questioning that she never tells them what to do; all the instructions are in her head.
      -- Facts about perceptions of self and other: "How did you expect he would react?" or, "What did you assume she thought?"
      -- Facts about perceptions of roles and models: "Who does

what in your house?" or, "How did your dad handle money?"
-- Facts about communication techniques:

"You weren't sure what he meant? What was it about his behavior that made you uncertain?"

"What did you say to him? What did you say back to her?"

"Did the words coming out of his mouth match the look on his face?"

"Did you try to get your point across? How? Then what did you do?"

-- Facts about how members express sexual feelings and act out. The therapist doesn't give double-level messages to patients to the effect that he really wants to hear about these subjects more than any other. His questions concern everyday living, including sex activities and periods of acting out. When discussing sexual material, the therapist does so in an open, concrete, matter-of-fact way. He treats this subject like any other. He says: "What way is it?" not, "Who is to blame?"; "How does that go?" not, "Why don't you respond?"

d. The therapist does not fear the patient is lying to him; he is not suspicious. He realizes the patient is not deliberately withholding information or misrepresenting it. He is responding to a vague fear of blame and low self-worth.

4. The therapist shows the patient how he looks to others.

   a. The therapist rises above the cultural prohibition against telling others how they manifest themselves:

      "Your nose is bleeding."

      "Your slip is showing."

      "You seem to want to be friends with him but you don't act the way you say you feel."

      "You seem to want to succeed but you act as though you might be afraid to try."

   b. The therapist realizes that people are grateful to be told how they manifest themselves.

      "We all need three-way mirrors. Yet we assume that others see in us what we feel we are manifesting."

      "We can give information if we do it in such a tone that

our good will is clear. Clarity of intent gets across if
our words, face, tone of voice, are all of a piece."

But such information must also be given in an appropriate context, in an appropriate relationship. The telling must not be
overdone, and good things must be told too. For example, a
husband had a glob of something on his shoe. He and his wife
sat through a whole therapy session with me. Finally the wife
mentioned it to her husband. He asked her why she hadn't told
him, and she said she didn't want to embarrass him or hurt
him. Also, she thought he knew about it. He was angry that
she hadn't told him. Even though the news we get from others
may be uncomfortable, we prefer that to not knowing the im-
pression we give.

  c. The therapist can also put the tape recorder to good use. Playing back tapes of previous conversations (which were openly
recorded, of course) can be a good way of showing people how
they sound and look to others, as well as making it easier for
patient and therapist to study the interactions of therapy. In
addition, the positive moves of patients can be pointed out to
them while playing back tapes.

5. When the therapist asks for and gives information, he does so in
a matter-of-fact, nonjudgmental, light, congruent way.

  a. The therapist verbally recreates situations in order to collect
facts. He has a flair for acceptance and imagination:

> Th: Now let me see. There was no bread. What did you
> do for bread that night?

> W: Well, we didn't have any.

> Th: Well, then you didn't get enough to eat. Now let's
> take a look at what you were trying to do. You wanted
> food on the table and it wasn't there. And you thought
> Harry was going to bring it. Your husband is telling
> you that you don't keep him informed, and you are
> telling him he doesn't care what happens in the house,
> what happens to you. Let's see where this all started.
> Here you are, Harry, coming in the door wondering
> if dinner's cooked. And your wife is thinking, "We
> don't have any bread..."

  b. By showing he is easy about giving and receiving information,
the therapist makes it easier for the patient to do so.
-- I can ask -- so can you.
-- I can give information -- so can you.
-- I can receive information -- so can you.
-- I can give a clear message -- so can you.

(But the therapist must beware of the inappropriate light touch. One time a trainee-therapist sat with a smile on her face while a patient was telling her about very painful material. The trainee's consultant-observer pointed this out to her after the session was over. She was unaware that she was doing this, and said she guessed she always smiled when things were painful to cover up what she was feeling inside. The therapist must be congruent in his behavior.)

6. The therapist builds self-esteem.

   a. The therapist makes constant "I value you" comments along the way:

      "You're a responsible person."

      "You have feelings too, you know."

      "You can want things for yourself, can't you?"

   b. The therapist labels assets. The patient is like a grocery store after an earthquake, with unlabeled goods lying all around. The therapist takes a tally for the patient; what is in stock, how it might be sold. The therapist says:

      "You showed you could do that quite well."

      "You never allowed yourself to develop that, did you?"

   c. The therapist asks the patient questions he can answer (see page 161).

   d. The therapist emphasizes that he and his patients are equals in learning.
     -- By asking questions, he tells his patients: "You contribute to what I know." (Family members check each other on facts and this should be encouraged.)
     -- He admits that he can make mistakes: "I goofed on that. I'm sorry," or, "I forgot. It was careless of me. I should have remembered."
     -- By his actions, he tells his patients, "I share what I know." The therapist shares as much of his assumptions and knowledge as he can, but at the right time and in an appropriate manner.

   e. The therapist includes himself as a person whose meaning can be checked on: "I will try to be perfectly clear. You check me if you don't follow me."

   f. The therapist takes the family's history and notes past achievements.

   g. The therapist begins to accentuate the idea of good intentions. but bad communication:

"I think Mother and Dad very much want to get across their messages, but somehow something seems to stand in their way."

"In this family I see everyone wanting to report on what they see and hear and on what they wish for, but somehow behaving as though others won't hear."

"There is no lack of good intentions, good wishes in this family. But somehow everyone seems to have trouble making these wishes clear."

"I don't think for a minute that anyone in this family wants to give pain to others. But when comments are made, they always seem to come out in the form of accusations."

"Why is it that members of this family don't seem able to give open reports to each other on what they see and hear?"

h. The therapist asks each family member what he can do that brings pleasure to another member:

"What can you do, Joe, that you know ahead of time will bring pleasure to Mary?" (and vice versa)

"What can you do, Johnny, that will bring big smiles to Mother's face?"

By these questions the therapist not only further delineates family rules, but he helps each member to see himself as others see him. Maybe Johnny says (about his father): "I can't do anything to please him." Maybe Joe says (about what he thinks his wife wants of him): "Just bring in the money." Maybe Mary says (about what Joe wants of her): "Just keep him fed."

i. The therapist is human, clear, direct. Love is not enough. The therapist works for maximum adaptability by helping the family to feel they are likeable. He raises their capacity to give and minimizes their sensitivities to painful subjects, thereby decreasing the necessity for defenses.

7. The therapist decreases threat by setting the rules of interaction.

a. The therapist sees to it that all are present: "We need your reaction, experience, on this," or, "Only you can tell us what you saw and heard."

b. He makes it clear that no one is to interrupt others:

"You're all talking at once. I can't hear."

"I guess Johnny will have to speak for five minutes, then Patty can speak for five minutes.

"You're hurting my eardrums."

c. He emphasizes that no one may act out or make it impossible to converse during the session:

"I have to hear in order to do my work."

"You got your point across. Now let's get to work."

"No wonder you have not been able to work this out. Nobody is listening to anybody else."

"Now I know how deeply you feel about this. There's no further need to show me."

"When you can talk in an adult manner, then come back and we'll get to work. Until then we will have to terminate therapy."

d. He makes sure that no one is allowed to speak for anybody else:

"When you speak, speak for yourself only."

"Let Johnny speak for himself. You can't be an authority on Johnny."

"Have you ever crawled inside another's skin and looked at a thought? You can't do it. Neither can I. We have to check."

"You can collect evidence on his behavior and on what he says and see if they fit. You can then ask about it. But only he can explain why his messages didn't fit."

"Did you ever ask what he meant by what he said? Or did you just guess?"

e. He tries to make everyone speak out clearly so he can be heard.

f. He makes direct requests to people to speak up:

"I'm a little deaf. Not very deaf, but a little deaf. You're going to have to speak up."

"We don't want to miss what you have to say."

"Maybe you feel that what you have to say isn't important."

g. He kids:

"Cat get your tongue?"

"Know the language?"

"You need practice in exercising that lower lip."

h. He relates silence to covert controls:'

"I saw you looking at Mother. Were you thinking she didn't want you to speak?"

"Maybe you think if you speak you'll get clobbered."

"We'll have to find out what makes it so unsafe to talk."

8. The therapist decreases threat by the way he structures the interviews:

a. The therapist announces that therapy is aiming toward a concrete goal and will have a definite end.
-- At the very beginning he sets boundaries: "This is not going to be an open-end process, one which may drag on indefinitely. The total number of interviews within which we shall try to work will be..."
-- He may also set more limited deadlines: "At the end of five sessions, we shall re-evaluate to see what has been accomplished, where we need to go."

b. The therapist plans the interviews so that the family will understand that he sees them as a <u>family</u> and is not taking anyone's side.
-- He may begin therapy by seeing the two mates, the "architects" of the family, or he may see the whole family together. But whenever he starts with a new family, he wants to see them all together at least once, even when the children are too young to enter therapy, in order to understand the operation of the family and what each person's place in it is.
-- He never sees the I. P. and his parents alone, as this would only reinforce the common assumption that the I. P. is the root of the family's trouble.
-- He never sees any unit other than the parents alone before he and the family are clear on the whole family's way of operating. Doing so before this understanding is reached may make the therapist appear to be in a coalition with certain family members, or getting privileged data which may be kept from other members. The therapist must guard against any actions which might be taken by the family as a

message about "who is to blame," "who is loved most,"
"who is sick," etc.

-- After the operation of the family is made explicit to the
therapist and the family, he can see individuals on a basis
understood by everyone to pertain to some work relating to
a marital pair, an individual, the sibling unit, and so forth.

-- The therapist singles out units when it seems practical or
feasible. Sometimes family members are away for business
or camp and seeing the separated units comes about naturally. If he sees anyone separately, it is always with the
idea of reporting back to the family group what he and they
have "discovered."

9. The therapist decreases threat by reducing the need for defenses.

   a. In my opinion, the dysfunctional family operates within a
      reign of terror, with all members fearing they will be hurt
      and all members fearing they will hurt others. All comments
      are taken as attacks on self-esteem. Therefore, the therapist
      must reduce terror. Defenses, as I seem them, are simply
      ways of enhancing self-esteem and defending against attacks
      on self-esteem. So the therapist does not have to "destroy"
      defenses in order to produce change. He exerts all his efforts
      to reducing terror, reducing the necessity for defenses.

   b. The therapist asks each family member what he can do that
      brings anger from another member:

      > "What can you do which you know, as sure as sure, will
      > make Dad blow his cork?"

      > "What can you do, Mary, that will make Joe especially
      > mad?"

   Such questions further delineate family rules and prohibitions.
   They help family members make covert rules overt. They also
   continue to decrease fears about showing anger.

   c. The therapist interprets anger as hurt:

      > "Well, as far as I am concerned, when a person looks
      > angry, this simply means he feels pain inside. In some
      > way he feels his self-esteem is in danger."

      > "We will have to work out ways so that you can all give
      > clear messages without feeling you will hurt other peo-
      > ple's feelings."

      > "Dad may look angry but he is really feeling some kind
      > of pain and hurt. He will have to give a clearer message
      > about his pain, so that others will know what is going on
      > inside him."

d. The therapist acknowledges anger as a defense and deals with the hurt:

    H: It's all I can do to keep from killing you!

    W: You're a mean old man!

    Th: Now I know how deeply disappointed you both are. Things have turned out so differently from what you hoped. Let's see what happened which has prevented the two of you from having joy and pleasure in your lives.

e. The therapist shows that pain and the forbidden are all right to look at:

    "Did you see your parents' pain? Were you able to relieve it?"

    "So your dad had a wooden leg. You couldn't talk about that, could you? That was painful for your family to talk about. Why?"

    "So Roger was adopted. Did you know this, Roger? What did Mother tell you about it? Why weren't you able, Mother, to tell Roger this?"

f. The therapist burlesques basic fears in the family:

    "Mother and Dad won't drop dead if you simply comment on what you see and hear."

    "You must think that Mother and Dad are pretty fragile creatures. They look like pretty strong people to me."

    "You seem to act, Mary, as if Joe will fall apart if you simply report on what you have observed."

By burlesquing, or by painting the picture ad absurdum, the therapist helps decrease overprotective feelings and feelings of omnipotence, thus further reducing the need for defenses.

10. The therapist decreases threat by handling loaded material with care.

a. He handles loaded material by careful timing, going from least-loaded to most-loaded.
    -- He goes from a history of the past, how couples first met, what they saw in each other, to the present interaction.
    -- He starts with a discussion about the parents of origin and leads on to a discussion about the present parents.

-- The timing of questions is done by the order in which they are asked during the history-taking:

"What did your parents do for fun?"

"How were your parents different from each other?"

"Were your parents able to disagree?"

"How did your parents disagree?"

"What do you do for fun?" etc.

b. The therapist switches to less loaded material when things get hot.
   -- To one subject rather than another (this depends on what in the family is the most loaded material).
   -- To the past rather than the present: "How did money-handling go in your family when you were a kid?"
c. The therapist handles loaded material by generalizing what one expects to see in families:

"It is not unusual for families to hurt, have pain, have problems, fight."

"When one person in a family is hurting (or angry, or frightened) all are feeling the same way."

"When one person in a family is hurting, all share a responsibility in that hurt."

d. The therapist handles loaded material by relating feelings to facts.
   -- He asks for specificity, examples, documentation: "He beats you sometimes? How often?" or, "He sort of cheats? What do you mean?"
   -- He asks about data that patients use to support their perceptions: "How do you know she doesn't care what you do?" or, "What does he do that makes you feel he is mean?
   -- But he does not ignore the real things to which patients are responding. He must be careful not to analyze a perception without checking it out against reality.
   -- Neither does he wallow in feeling or allow others to do so. He must also keep from analyzing feelings separate from the context of interaction.
e. He handles loaded material by using his own personal idiom.
   -- He uses slang: "Dad hit the ceiling then, huh? or, "I guess the fur flew then."
   -- He uses profanity, vulgarity: "All right. So he acted like a bastard that time," or, "You must have been mad as hell."
   -- He avoids pedantic words and psychiatric jargon. He uses

"self-esteem" instead of "poor sex identity"; "count" and and "valued" instead of "acceptable"; "lovable" instead of "loved," etc.

f. He handles loaded material by translating hostile behavior and feelings:

> "So you felt unlovable."

> "So you felt attacked."

> "So what came out of your mouth didn't match the pain inside. How come?"

g. He handles loaded material by preventing closure on episodes and complaints (besides, he often has insufficient data from which to evaluate what feelings are about): "As we go along this will become clearer," or, "We can learn more about that."

11. Let us now move forward to seeing how the therapist re-educates patients for adulthood, for accountability.

a. The patient constantly gives clues that he does not feel accountable:

> "I can't do it." (I am little, insignificant.)

> "They won't let me do it." (Others are bigger than I am. I am a victim.)

> "You made me do it." (I fix accountability in you.)

> "Yes, I do it, but can't help it. I don't know why." (I fix accountability inside me, but I am not related to myself.)

> "I did it because I was drunk (amnesic, crazy).' (I was not me.)

> "I didn't mean to do it." (I was not me.)

> "I did it because I love you." (Blackmail Syndrome.)

b. The therapist uses certain techniques for restoring the patient's feeling of accountability.
-- He reminds the patient of his ability to be in charge of himself:

> "Who eats for you?"

> "Who goes to the toilet for you?"

"You can decide, you know."

"You don't have to rob yourself, you know." (To a patient who wants to quit school.)

"How did it happen, if you didn't mean to do it?"

"Others can't see your inside wish. They can only see the outward behavior which gives a clue to the wish. You have to make your wishes clear."

"You invested that person with authority over you. Why did you give your authority away?"

"You made an agreement with him that he would control you. Does this have to go on?"

"What stands between you and your ability to control Mary?"

-- The therapist checks back always on pronouns to see who did what to whom. Schizophrenics, for instance, never say exactly who did what. They say: "Children shouldn't do such and such." The therapist pins the patient down: "You mean Johnnie?" The therapist makes the patient's covert accusations overt so that they can be dealt with and so that he can check if the pronouns are accurately placed.

-- The therapist deals with tattletalers:

S: (to mother) I'm going to tell on you.

Th: Now I think you want to get Ma in trouble. Does this happen at home? How come you parents are in a position where your kids can get one of you in trouble?

* * * * * * *

M: My husband drinks.

Th: (turns attention to what wife can report on herself) Do you drink?

* * * * * * *

D: (discrepancy watcher) He gets ten cents. I only get five cents.

Th: You want to make sure you get your share of things. That you don't get robbed or left out.

-- The therapist deals with spokesmen:

> "How does it happen that you have to be a spokes-
> man for Johnny? He can speak for himself. Let's
> ask him about this."

> "Does this go on at home? People speaking for other
> people? How do you suppose this came to be?"

    -- The therapist deals with acting-out of children (see page
    166 for acting-out of adults). He doesn't turn to the parents •
    He asks the child, "How come?" He reminds the child that
    he has a choice about his behavior. He isn't a victim. He
    can influence his environment.

c. The patient-therapist relationship itself highlights problems
   of accountability.

    -- The patient behaves in a certain way. He acts as if he is
    stuck with that behavior, can't help it. If the therapist, too,
    treats this behavior as separate from the person, he is say-
    ing to the patient, "I expect you to have no controls." So
    he highlights the behavior as belonging to the person, and
    he sets up behavior treatment goals.

    -- The patient expects the therapist to be a great white father
    or mother from whom all things flow. He expects the thera-
    pist to take charge. The therapist does take charge, but
    does not treat the patient like a child or expect him to be-
    have like one. He treats the patient like an adult and expects
    him to behave like an adult. He does not violate the adult
    label.

    -- The therapist is not indispensable to the patient, though he
    may need to think he is. He is not like the parent of the
    schizophrenic who says: "You can't feed yourself. You
    need me to live." So he doesn't give to patients in a "feed-
    ing" and "draining" kind of way. He only makes it possible
    for them to give to themselves and get from other family
    members.

12. The therapist helps the patient to see how past models influence
his expectations and behavior (see page 105).

a. He reminds patients that they are acting from past models:

> "I would expect you to be worried about that. As you
> said, your dad never..."

> "Your mother handled money that way. How could you
> have learned other ways?"

> "Now it sounds to me as if you are giving the same kind
> of message to him that you saw your mother give to
> your dad. Yet you didn't like the way your mother and
> father handled things and are struggling hard to do it
> differently. Let's see what may be standing in your way."

b. The therapist openly challenges expectations: "Do you really believe that all children should be beholden to their parents?"

c. The therapist reminds patients that they married each other for the very qualities about which they are now complaining. "Now this is what you said you liked about your wife. I wonder why you don't like it now?"

d. The therapist highlights expectations by completing communication:

> Th: (to Johnny) Do you like spinach?
>
> S: No.
>
> Th: Did you know your mother thought you did like spinach?
>
> S: No, but I didn't want to hurt her feelings.
>
> Th: (to mother) Did you ever ask him if he liked spinach
>
> M: No, I thought all men did. Pa did.

e. The therapist highlights expectations by exaggerating them: "Your Pa did it, so naturally all men do it!"

13. The therapist delineates roles and functions.

a. The therapist recognizes roles himself, in addressing and treating a family.
   -- He calls couples "Mother" and "Dad" when referring to them as parents and by their first names when referring to them as individuals or as husband and wife.
   -- In history-taking, the therapist includes members in a relevant order. He takes the father first, as head of the house, and next, the mother. He then takes the oldest sib first, saying to the younger ones: "Wait a minute. You haven't arrived yet. You haven't been born!"

b. The therapist questions patients about their roles:

> "You wear three hats -- individual, marital, parental. I can see the parental, but where are the other two?"
>
> "Before marriage you were Miss So-and-So. What happened to her?"
>
> "Why do you have to get permission?"
>
> "Are you Daddy's wife?"

c. The therapist can teach explicitly about roles. He lists three

roles on the blackboard: individual, marital, parental. He
does this so that patients will see that they have a choice as to
how they will treat each other. If the therapist makes patients
aware of how they are responding and shows them other ways
to respond, they can then choose among these ways. Creativity
in living is having a wider choice of alternatives.

14. The therapist completes gaps in communication and interprets
messages.

   a. The therapist separates the relationship part of a message
   from its content. Patients usually confuse the two and talk
   about relationships in "content" terms:
   -- "This coffee is no good" is a patient's way of saying, "You
   are no good."
   -- "Glasses get dirty" is a schizophrenic's way of saying, "You
   can't see straight."

   b. The therapist separates comments about the self from comments about others. Patients usually confuse the two, and
   can't figure out which part of an interchange tells them something about the speaker and which part is addressed to them.
   -- "I'm tired" can be a statement about the speaker's fatigue.
   It can also be a question: "You too?" It can also be a request: "Help me!"
   -- So when the patient tells the therapist what B said, the
   therapist asks what the patient got out of B's message.

   c. The therapist points out significant discrepancies in communication:

   > F: I feel fine.

   > Th: You look awful. How come you say you feel fine
   > when you look awful. Can't you allow yourself to
   > feel like Hell?

   * * * * * * *

   > F: (to child, whose symptom is related to the father's
   > delinquent behavior) Be good and I'll be back soon.

   > Th: (to father) I think there were two parts to that mes-
   > sage which perhaps confused her. You said to be
   > good very loud and clear, but you did not tell her
   > where you were going and when you would be back.
   > Did the second message come through equally loud
   > and clear?

   d. The therapist spells out nonverbal communication:

   > Th: (to Johnny) You looked to your mother first, before
   > answering. I wonder if you feel you have to get per-
   > mission to speak.

Th: (To Patty, who takes her father's hand during an argument between her mother and father) Are you telling your dad that you sympathize with him?

* * * * * * *

Th: (in reference to seating pattern) You all act as though you would like to get as far away from him (me, her) as possible.

e. The therapist spells out "double-level" messages:

D: (to mother) May I go to school?

M: (to daughter) When I was a little girl, I never had an education.

Th: (to mother) Now your daughter asked you if she could go to school and I'm wondering if she got an answer from you. Should she go to school or shouldn't she?

15. In general, here are my criteria for terminating treatment.

a. Treatment is completed:
   -- When family members can complete transactions, check, ask.
   -- When they can interpret hostility.
   -- When they can see how others see them.
   -- When they can see how they see themselves.
   -- When one member can tell another how he manifests himself.
   -- When one member can tell another what he hopes, fears, and expects from him.
   -- When they can disagree.
   -- When they can make choices.
   -- When they can learn through practice.
   -- When they can free themselves from harmful effects of past models.
   -- When they can give a clear message, that is, be congruent in their behavior, with a minimum of difference between feelings and communication, and with a minimum of hid-- den messages.

b. Another set of criteria for terminating treatment is when the adult male and female as husband and wife can:
   -- Be direct, using the first person "I" and following with state- ments or questions which:

Criticize	Find fault
Evaluate	Report annoyance
Acknowledge an observation	Identify being puzzled

-- <u>Be delineated</u>, by using language which clearly shows "I am me" and "You are you." "I am separate and apart from you and I acknowledge my own attributes as belonging to me. You are you, separate and apart from me, and I acknowledge your attributes as belonging to you."
-- <u>Be clear</u>, by using questions and statements which reflect directness and the capacity to get knowledge of someone else's statements, directions, or intentions, in order to accomplish an outcome.

c. In short, treatment is completed when everyone in the therapy setting can use the first person "I" followed by an active verb and ending with a direct object.

Chapter XV

Integrating Models and Disciplines

1. Family therapy is just over ten years old and already new models are emerging, which I consider to be a sign of health in any behavioral science. Although I have described my personal conceptions and practices in this book on family therapy, I do not wish the reader to see it as just another rigid model which cannot be altered or varied. I have tried to cut through the barriers between disciplines, forms, and models, and take a look at the basic process which occurs in all relationships involving human beings, with particular emphasis laid on the therapeutic and family relationships.

2. There is nothing sacred in a formula or model. The important thing is always the understanding and use of the formula in the here and now. Form is not the same as process.

   a. Process implies movement. It is dynamic, not static.
   b. Process focuses not on the activity per se, but on the carrying on of the activity.
   c. Process is more a matter of "how" than of "what"; form and content are more matters of "what" than of "how."
   d. One of the reasons why diagnostic labels are damaging is that they easily become self-fulfilling prophecies, tending to freeze process into outcome.
   e. Process avoids dichotomies, since a person can be X at one moment in time and Y at another moment.
   f. Process is best described in verbs ending in -ing.

3. The basic process which occurs in every relationship, regardless of content, structure, or form, is:

   a. an encounter
   b. between two people
   c. at a particular moment in time.

4. The future of human relations disciplines and modalities lies in the integration of their various partial views of man in relation to the four basic parts of the self, which are:

a. the mind
b. the body
c. the report of the senses (the interaction between mind and body), and
d. interaction with others (social relationships).

5. All of us operate within multiple relationship systems, and our self-concepts and self-images are derived from the context of the system we are in at any particular moment in time. This means that identity is dynamic, constantly changing, and the individual has myriad potentialities and contingency possibilities that are only neglected through prohibitions and sanctions preventing self-exploration and change. The limited individual has a limited self-image, which he derives from a limited context that prevents growth.

6. If one approaches therapy from an integrational viewpoint, it becomes clear that many fields not labeled as "human relations" disciplines had much to say about parts of the human gestalt long before human relations fields emerged. In my therapy and training, I make use of principles and ideas gleaned from the disciplines of dance, drama, religion, medicine, communications, education, speech, the behavioral sciences — even the physical sciences, from which the "systems concept" (on which my practice is based) first derived.* Integration, in theory and practice, of all the tools available to man for his growth is necessary before we begin to deal in fact with the "total man."

7. The management relations field, like family therapy, is showing a trend toward increasing use of the systems concept. Recently, two University of Michigan researchers, Rummler and Brethower, raised certain basic questions about management personnel factors that are relevant to the theory being proposed here.** 1Rummler and Brethower feel that the trend in management relations is toward behavioral technology based on classifying behavior problems into supervisory, training, and systems problems. They are beginning to deal with the worker in the "here and now" and to utilize many new learning techniques, emphasizing the extreme importance of reinforcement in helping the worker adapt to new patterns. The trend is away from personality and morale checklists and assessment of motivation and needs. It is interesting to note the similarity between these authors' ideas and the movement in family therapy away from traditional models toward more systems concepts and programmed

---

*For a complete explanation of the systems concept, see Watzlawick, P., Beavin, J., and Jackson, D., *Pragmatics of Human Communication*, New York: W. W. Norton, 1967.

***The Social Science Reporter and Public Relations Research Review*, Vol. XV, No. 5, May 1967, Palo Alto, California.

behavior in which the individual learns to deal with his "job" or various roles in the here and now, and receives appropriate reinforcement to keep his knowledge live and current.

8. This type of training has not penetrated traditional psychoanalytic theory and practice to any extent. While many disciplines are concerned with updating their efforts to improve human functioning, psychoanalysis and much of the field of psychiatry are struggling to defend their original precepts and practices.

9. Proscribed, rigid psychotherapeutic practices are inadequate to meet the constantly changing growth needs of human beings. The truth of this statement is obvious from the points I have stressed throughout this book, namely:

    a. the need for the individual to observe himself in interaction, including the part he plays in the family system,

    b. the need to realize how his behavior and self-concept is circumscribed by the system itself, and

    c. the need for therapeutic reinforcement to make this knowledge available to family members and help them experience and practice new interactional behaviors.

10. In my own treatment sessions, I (like many others in the field) set virtually no limits on the behaviors which are possible to meet the needs of the moment.

    a. I range from an intake interview that may last an hour and a half to sessions which last several or more hours. More recently, I have relied increasingly on "marathon" sessions, which means spending a weekend or longer with one or several families in order to have continuous contact in a variety of contexts. In other words, time is flexible and variable.

    b. I see families and individuals in my office, outdoors, in their homes, in their places of work and recreation; i.e., anyplace it seems likely that we can experience new contexts and relationships. I visit the school and nursery, if indicated. In short, place is flexible and variable.

    c. Once I have seen the family together enough to have a good, comprehensive understanding of the total family system, I often see a particular family member in an individual session, or see certain family dyads or triads, or shift sessions from seeing one or two at a time to seeing the whole family together again, often in a single interview. I vary the sessions according to the need and my analysis of the family system. Often, I see more than one family together. In other words, the pattern of persons seen is flexible and variable.

    d. At times, I find it helpful to utilize a co-therapist or more than one co-therapist, either of the same sex or the opposite sex. Therefore, the pattern of therapists involved is flexible and variable.

e. In addition to varying techniques and time patterns, I use many invaluable mechanical aids in therapy and training. I use the tape recorder and the Polaroid camera to give instant feedback, or review earlier interactional episodes, or take a picture of the person who doubts that he looks angry or depressed or is giving other unconscious, nonverbal messages to others in interaction. I use the audio-visual TV tape for the same purposes and for the additional advantage of permitting the family to hear and see themselves at the same time. I have increasingly relied on dancing, body movement exercises, drama, and games in order to provide the family with varying experiences in touching, seeing, hearing, feeling, and expressing. In short, techniques and tools for experiencing are are flexible and variable.

11. Naturally, none of these techniques has been established as "ideal" or "the most desirable," and many new aids other than those I have described will doubtless be developed in the future. The important point is that whatever techniques are used, the focus should be on providing a new growth experience for the family or the individual. This means that the therapist must be a person and a peer to the family and not a godlike figure who tries to hold himself aloof from the relationship system.

12. The therapeutic modus operandi, which governs how much the therapist permits himself to become involved and in what way, depends heavily on the therapist's models and beliefs about:

a. what causes illness,
b. what makes illness go away, and
c. what makes people grow.

13. One can visualize today's psychotherapy as being based on one of three models:

a. the medical model,
b. the sin model, or
c. the growth model.

14. In the medical model, the cause of illness is believed to have its locus in the patient himself. It is believed that the illness is removed by destroying its source within the patient. Growth is expected to occur spontaneously once the cause of the illness is removed, thereby releasing pent-up energy for growth. In this model, the use of touch or closeness by the therapist is irrelevant, since the problem is within the patient. The psychoanalytic model is a perfect example of the medical model because here the patient lies on the couch, speaks from his "innermost" mind, and does not even have eye contact with the therapist. If the analyst adheres strictly to "non-directive, patient-oriented" techniques, even verbal contact is strictly limited. The assumption

is that "I, the therapist, do nothing to stimulate you, so every-thing you feel and do is inherent in you." Since, however, it is impossible <u>not</u> to communicate, this assumption is a myth.

15. In the sin model, it is believed that something is wrong with the patient's thinking, values, and attitudes which requires changing. "Cure" is thought to occur when the patient has developed new values—unavoidably based on the therapist's values. One might say, in the words of Don Jackson, that in the sin model the patient is "cured" when he learns to utilize the same labels as the therapist. Growth is expected to occur once the patient's values and attitudes are "corrected," regardless of whether he has had any training or experience whatsoever in the behaviors necessary to put the new attitudes into practice. The sin model is a "should not" system and presumes that the therapist knows what the patient should do and become.

16. The growth model is based on the notions that people's behavior changes through process and that the process is represented by transactions with other people. Illness is believed to be an appropriate communicative response to a dysfunctional system or context. It is therefore believed that illness goes away when the individual is removed from the maladaptive system or the system is changed to permit healthy responses and communication. Growth occurs when the system permits it. The therapist, being an integral part of the therapeutic system, is intimately involved in the transactions, and anything he may offer the patient or patients to expedite learning and exchange (touching, holding hands, asking the patient to do him a favor, sitting together comfortably as peers do) is utilized to help the patient grow within the context of the relationship.

17. If one uses the growth model, he must be willing to be more experimental and spontaneous than many therapists are. The necessity of flexibility in technique and approach, including particularly direct, intimate contact between patient and therapist, is thought to be basic.

   a. In growth therapy, techniques are not utilized to accomplish specific goals, such as increasing the father's yearly earnings or making sure that junior goes to college.
   b. Growth therapy is based on the premise that people can be taught to be congruent, to speak directly and clearly, and to communicate their feelings, thoughts, and desires accurately in order to be able to deal with what is.

18. To compare these models in action, let us imagine, for example, that a patient were to ask the therapist how he himself has fun.

   a. In the medical model, the question would be considered irrelevant.

b. In the sin model, the question would be considered impertinent.

c. In the growth model, the question would be considered a legitimate request for information.

19. In the growth model, the therapist makes the point by his own behavior that there is nothing which cannot be dealt with openly and honestly, nor is there any substitute in therapy or any human relationship for a human being's learning to use himself and his own personality—not only using himself to influence others but, when appropriate, letting go and being influenced by others.

20. The therapist, because he is a person intimately involved in the relationship system, provides an example for growth, either positively or negatively. The problems in the medical and sin models with regard to setting a healthy example are obvious.

   a. The vision presented by the traditional analyst is that of withdrawal, non-involvement, non-commitment, and the virtual elimination of looking, talking, and touching as effective means of communication in relationship.

   b. In the sin model, the therapist becomes a living example of the worried, disapproving, or critical parent who in many cases drove the patient into therapy in the first place. By sanctioning limited, idiosyncratic values, he presents a narrow vision of potential, "acceptable" growth patterns for his inquiring patient.

   c. In the growth model, the therapist sets the example of an active, learning, fallible human being who is willing to cope honestly and responsibly with whatever confronts him, including his own vulnerabilities.

21. In order to learn and to demonstrate what happens to an individual's behavior when he operates within the context of one of the three models described, I have in recent years made increasing use of games—both in family therapy and in training professionals in various human relations disciplines. The major games I have developed for this purpose are:

   a. The simulated family,
   b. family systems games, and
   c. communication games.

The Simulated Family

1. The Bateson group, working in Palo Alto in 1954, came upon the notion that families are constrained by redundant behavioral patterns that occur over and over again outside of the family's awareness. In attempting to demonstrate this by utilizing role-playing among the members of the group (Bateson, Jackson, Haley, and Weakland), they were surprised to find themselves

developing strong feelings in relation to the behaviors they were
merely acting out in the role of a particular "family" member.
Further, they were able to show that, by following certain simple
rules, they could simulate, for example, the family of a chronic
schizophrenic patient to such a degree that the recording of these
sessions sent for "blind" diagnosis to various other investigators
in the country was considered to be a tape of a real schizophrenic
family. Even the voices of the researchers (who were well known
to the other investigators) were not recognized, although no voice
change had been intended by the so-called "role-players."

2. I have had experience now with utilizing "simulated family" techniques with hundreds of different audiences and with many different professional groups, from physicians to social workers,
teachers, and nurses. One comment should be made about the
use of games for training purposes. A common reaction of professionals who have not participated in such games is that it is
just "role-playing" and therefore unreal. In all of my experience
in using these games with many groups across the country, I
have never encountered a person who did not, once involved in a
game system, develop vivid "gut reactions" to the roles he
played, particularly those roles which are contrary to his own
self-image. It is very common for someone to say, after a particular game, "Now I know how Mrs. X feels and can sympathize
with her ulcer problem! This sounds just like her. After five minutes of it, my own stomach is churning."

3. On one memorable occasion, a young social worker played the
identified-patient daughter in a particular simulated family, while
a general physician, interested in family therapy, was her simulated father. At the end of about 40 minutes of family interaction,
the "daughter" stood up, threw her arms around the older man
and stated, "I really love you!" and he, with tears streaming
down his face, stated, "It's the first time I have ever really felt
what I missed in not having a daughter."

4. Naturally, the technique of the simulated family is not used only
to teach therapists but is invaluable in teaching real families
about themselves. This can be done in two primary ways:

   a. The therapist can have family members simulate each other's
   behaviors. For example, mother may behave as she thinks
   father does, while father may play the part of his daughter,
   and the son may act out his conception of his mother's behavior.

   b. The therapist can have the family members play themselves
   in a simulated situation, i.e., one that the therapist constructs
   from his understanding of their particular family system. For
   example, in a scapegoating family, the members may be required to act out a drama in which they are to pretend they
   are a different family, one in which little Johnny is the fa-

vorite. Mother is the one who is always being picked on by the other family members, and she puts up with it by being a martyr. The family can then be made acquainted with their behavior by the use of audio-visual tape, which is played back to them, and both family and therapist discuss how different or how similar various family members' behaviors were in relation to their usual behaviors.

Systems Games:

1. A very useful tool for both training and therapy is what I call "family systems games." I developed these on the basis of my observation over a period of time that all interactional systems can be classified as either open systems or closed systems.

   a. Closed systems are those in which every participating member must be very cautious about what he or she says. The principal rule seems to be that everyone is supposed to have the same opinions, feelings, and desires, whether or not this is true. In closed systems, honest self-expression is impossible, and if it does occur, the expression is viewed as deviant or "sick" or "crazy" by the other members of the group or family. Differences are treated as dangerous, a situation that results in one or more members having to figuratively "be dead to themselves" if they are to remain in the system. The limitations placed on individual growth and health in such a group is obvious, and I have found that emotional or behavioral disturbance is a certain sign that the disturbed person is a member of a closed family system.
   b. An open system permits honest self-expression for the participating members. In such a group or family, differences are viewed as natural, and open negotiation occurs to resolve such differences by "compromise," "agreement to disagree," "taking turns," etc. In open systems, the individual can say what he feels and thinks and can negotiate for reality and personal growth without destroying himself or the others in the system.

2. Through use of four basic "rules" of interactional patterns played by the original family triad (father, mother, and child) or by trainees taking these roles, I discovered that it is possible to simulate almost any family system, closed or open, and to learn in the process.

   a. The first interactional rule dictates that a person is to handle differences by eliminating himself. In other words, he always agrees with others in the system regardless of how he really feels.
   b. The second rule is that one may handle differences by eliminating the others, by always disagreeing, finding fault, and blaming.

    c. In the third rule, one eliminates both self and other by always being irrelevant, changing the subject, etc., so that both self and other find it impossible to openly negotiate differences.

    d. The fourth rule permits the inclusion of both self and other in the system, i.e., a person negotiates openly and clearly and permits others to do the same.

3. On the basis of these four rules, I devised four sets of games to simulate, by shifting the component parts, any system of interaction.

    a. The first set is called <u>rescue games</u>, in which rules number one, two, and three are played, i.e., one member of the original family triad always agrees, one always disagrees, and the third is always irrelevant. In most interactional systems, the same person plays by the same rule most of the time. Who plays by which rule is variable—i.e., Father can be the agreer, Mother the disagreer, and the child, the subject-changer; or Mother can be the irrelevant one, the child the agreer, and Father the disagreer. This pattern of interaction is very common in families which produce a schizophrenic member.

    b. The second set of games is called <u>coalition games</u>, which are based on rules one and two. In other words, two people always agree and the third disagrees or two disagree and one agrees. The implications for people caught in this game are obvious. It requires some "disturbed behavior" in order for a person to disagree with two people when one of those is agreeing and one is disagreeing, or for a person to agree with two people who are disagreeing, etc.

    c. The third set of games, called <u>lethal games</u>, is made up completely of rule one. In such a system, everyone agrees with everyone else, at the expense of his own needs and satisfactions. This is a common interactional pattern in families which develop a high incidence of psychosomatic illness.

    d. The fourth set of games is composed entirely of rule four, which I call <u>growth vitality games</u>. In such a system, each person includes self and others in interaction by expressing himself and also permitting others to express themselves.

4. It is obvious that the <u>growth vitality game</u> does not exist on the same level as the first three games. The first three games are survival games, and the fourth simply occurs on the <u>content reality level</u> rather than on the survival level. In such a game, people can <u>either</u> agree <u>or</u> disagree, in accordance with their experiential reality, and still remain a part of the system.

5. I use these games in treatment and in training. They are invaluable in three major ways:

    a. They help real or simulated "families" to see and understand the nature of their own family system.

b. They permit the family and the trainee to experience <u>new</u> interactional patterns (while experiencing new behaviors in their individual reaction patterns).

c. By having a family play the full sequence of games, they can not only identify where they <u>are</u> but also where it is possible to go. By making the systems explicit and ending with a "growth vitality game," families and professional trainees can <u>experience</u> the <u>movement</u> from a pathological system of interaction to a growth-producing one.

6. These games are not fixed and invariable. Within the general framework, the parts and variables can be shifted and rearranged to suit the needs of the occasion.

a. Instructions are usually necessary, such as assigning the roles and describing what the participants must do (e. g. , to always agree with whatever is said without using the words "I agree"). I usually assign a task for the group to carry out, such as, "Plan something you can do together as a family. " From there on, they carry the ball any way they can.

b. Sometimes I join in as a participant; sometimes, I observe. Sometimes, I interrupt or give new instructions, whispered to individuals or aloud to the whole family. Sometimes, I whisper a switch in role to one member, so the family can see what happens to a system when one member changes his rules of behavior without advising the other members.

c. Of course, it is of great importance that the family discuss their feelings and thoughts and reactions during and/or after the game. Strong emphasis is placed on "gut feelings," i. e., the physical, body reactions to the role being played. For example, when an individual must always agree, he may experience body tenseness, tight stomach, deep anger, etc. One who "always disagrees" may experience body heat, shaking, and headache. The "irrelevant one" may feel "crazy as a loon. "

Communication Games:

1. The third major category of games I have developed is a series of various interactional techniques that are great for teaching people to communicate more effectively and congruently. To date, the <u>communication games</u> have been used primarily with dyads, but it is not difficult to imagine expanding the idea to incorporate varied operational techniques.

2. I hit upon these games due to my repeated observation that when a person delivers an incongruent or mixed message, he or she usually is "out of touch" with the listener, in that little skin and eye contact occurs. I discovered after some experimentation that people find it almost impossible to send out an incongruent message if they have skin and/or steady eye contact with the listener.

In my efforts to teach my patients and trainees to improve their communications, I developed the following techniques. They are meant to be used generally as a series of interactions, to show people concretely and experientially what happens when they do or do not look, touch, and speak in a congruent manner.

 a. I place two persons (mother and father, father and child, two trainees, etc.) back to back and ask them to talk. This is similar in form to some communications at home, with the wife in the kitchen cooking while her husband tries to discuss finances with her.

 b. Then I turn them around face to face and have them "eyeball" each other without touching or talking. A great deal is learned when discussing this interaction, about the assumptions a person makes about the other's thoughts and feelings, when communication is verbally and sensorily constrained.

 c. I then have the couple "eyeball" and touch each other without talking.

 d. They then are asked to touch (e.g., hold hands) with their eyes closed and without talking.

 e. They then "eyeball" and talk without touching.

 f. Finally, I have the couple talk and touch and "eyeball" and try to argue with each other. They find that it is impossible. They either enjoy the effort or are forced to pull back physically and divert their eyes to get angry. It is also very difficult to deliver an incongruent message when one is talking, touching, and looking at the listener.

3. The most important part of these games is the therapist's interventions and the discussions during and after the series, about the couple's feelings, responses, and gut (bodily) reactions in relation to themselves, the other, and the interaction itself.

4. A final variation I will describe here is what I call the "blind walk." This technique involves having one person (e.g., the wife) take another (husband, child, etc.) on a walk while the second party keeps his or her eyes closed. I ask the person "in charge" to make the walk as interesting as possible (for example, having the "blind" person sit, stand, feel objects, etc.) and to use his/her body freely to direct the partner without possible injury. They are not permitted to talk during the walk. Afterwards, we discuss their feelings — fears, doubts, sense of trust, enjoyment, etc. For couples with serious "trust" and "dependence" problems in their relationship, this game can be particularly useful.

5. All of the games described (which will be elaborated in a future book) can be helpful or useless in therapy, depending on the ability of the therapist to enter into the relationship system openly and flexibly. He must, above all, show the enthusiasm and personal commitment necessary to engage his patients in the

spirit of learning, experimentation, and serious appraisal necessary to make the games a vivid new experience in interaction

6. I repeat once again that these games are not to be reified or labeled as techniques applicable only in the "innovative freedom of sunny California." They can be added to, abbreviated, or revised in accordance with the therapist's idiosyncratic personality and his clients' particular needs, problems, and wishes. They are the forms, not the process, of therapy. The process still— and always—is the relationship between you and me, here and now

Bibliography

1. Ackerman, N.W. Interpersonal disturbances in the family: Some unsolved problems in psychotherapy. Psychiatry, 17: 359-368, 1954.
2. Ackerman, N.W. A changing conception of personality — a personal viewpoint. Amer. J. Psychoanal., 17: 78-86, 1957.
3. Ackerman, N.W. An orientation to psychiatric research on the family. Marr. & Fam. Living, 19: 68-74, 1957.
4. Ackerman, N.W. Behavior trends and disturbances of the contemporary family. In I. Galdston (Ed.), The Family in Contemporary Society. New York: Int. Univ. Press, 1958.
5. Ackerman, N.W. The Psychodynamics of Family Life. New York: Basic Books, 1958.
6. Ackerman, N.W. Discussion of Hasting's paper, "Professional Staff Morale." In S.C. Sher and H.R. Davis (Eds.), The Out-Patient Treatment of Schizophrenia. New York: Grune & Stratton, 1960.
7. Ackerman, N.W. Family-focused therapy of schizophrenics. In S.C. Sher and H.R. Davis (Eds.), The Out-Patient Treatment of Schizophrenia. New York: Grune & Stratton, 1960.
8. Ackerman, N.W. The schizophrenic patient and his family relationships, a conceptual basis for family-focused therapy of schizophrenia. In M. Greenblatt, D.J. Levinson, and G.L. Klerman (Eds.) Mental Patients in Transition, Steps in Hospital-Community Rehabilitation. Springfield, Ill.: Thomas, 1961.
9. Ackerman, N.W. Family psychotherapy and psychoanalysis: Implications of difference. Fam. Proc., 1: 30-43, 1962.
10. Ackerman, N.W. Treating the Troubled Family. New York: Basic Books, 1966.
11. Ackerman, N.W., Beatman, F.L., and Sherman, S.N. (Eds.) Exploring the Base for Family Therapy. New York: Family Service Association of America, 1961.
12. Alanen, Y. Some thoughts on schizophrenia and ego development in the light of family investigations. Arch. gen. Psychiat., 3: 650-656, 1960.
13. Albert, Robert S. Stages of breakdown in relationships and dynamics between the mental patient and his family. Arch. gen. Psychiat., 3: 682-690, 1960.
14. Altman, C.H. Relationships between maternal attitudes and child personality structure. Amer. J. Orthopsychiat., 28: 160-169, 1958.

This bibliography represents an extended reading list pertaining to the family therapy approach, and is included for readers interested in widening their knowledge of this new field.

15. Appel, K. E.; Goodwin, H. M.; Wood, H. P., and Askren, E. L. Training in psychotherapy, the use of marriage counseling in a university teaching clinic. Amer. J. Psychiat., 117:709-711, 1961.

16. Arieti, S. Schizophrenia: the manifest symptomatology, the psychodynamic and formal mechanisms. In S. Arieti (Ed.), American Handbook of Psychiatry. New York: Basic Books, 1959.

17. Arieti, S. Discussion of Ackerman's paper, "Family-focused therapy of schizophrenia." In S.C. Sher and H.R. Davis (Eds.) The Out-Patient Treatment of Schizophrenia. New York: Grune & Stratton, 1960.

18. Arieti, S. Recent conceptions and misconceptions of schizophreni Amer. J. Psychother., 14: 3-29, 1960.

19. Asch, S. E. Studies of independence and conformity: a minority of one against a unanimous majority. Psychol. Monogr., 70: 1-70, 1956.

20. Bateson, G. A theory of play and fantasy. Psychiat. Res. Rep., 2: 39-51, 1955.

21. Bateson, G. Analysis of group therapy in an admission ward. In H. A. Wilmer (Ed.), Social Psychiatry in Action. Springfield, Ill.: Thomas, 1958.

22. Bateson, G. Language and psychotherapy, Frieda Fromm-Reichmann's last project. Psychiatry, 21: 96-100, 1958.

23. Bateson, G. Naven, 2nd edition with a new chapter. Stanford Univ. Press, 1958.

24. Bateson, G. Schizophrenic distortion of communication. In C. Whitaker (Ed.), Psychotherapy of Chronic Schizophrenic Patients. Boston: Little, Brown, 1958.

25. Bateson, G. Anthropological theories. Science, 129: 334-349, 1959.

26. Bateson, G. Cultural problems posed by a study of schizophrenic process. In A. Auerback (Ed.), Schizophrenia, an Integrated Approach. New York: Ronald Press, 1959.

27. Bateson, G. Panel review. In J.H. Masserman (Ed.), Individual and Familial Dynamics. New York: Grune & Stratton, 1959.

28. Bateson, G. Discussion of Samuel J. Beck's "Families of schizophrenic and of well children; method, concepts and some results. Amer. J. Psychiat., 30: 263-266, 1960.

29. Bateson, G. The group dynamics of schizophrenia. In L. Appleby J. M. Scher, and J. Cumming (Eds.), Chronic Schizophrenia: Explorations in Theory and Treatment. Glencoe, Ill.: Free Press 1960.

30. Bateson, G. Minimal requirements for a theory of schizophrenia. Arch. gen. Psychiat., 2: 477-491, 1960.

31. Bateson, G. The biosocial integration of behavior in the schizophrenic family. In N.W. Ackerman, F.L. Beatman, and S. Sanford (Eds.), Exploring the Base for Family Therapy. New York: Family Service Assoc., 1961.

32. Bateson, G. The challenge of research in family diagnosis and therapy, summary of panel discussion: I. Formal research in family structure. In N.W. Ackerman; F.L. Beatman, and S.

Sanford (Eds.), Exploring the Base for Family Therapy. New York: Family Service Assn., 1961.

33. Bateson, G. (Ed.) Perceval's Narrative, a Patient's Account of His Psychosis, 1830-1832. Stanford Univ. Press, 1961.

34. Bateson, G.; Jackson, D.D.; Haley, J., and Weakland, J.H. A note on the double bind -- 1962. Fam. Proc., 2: 154-161, 1963.

35. Bateson, G.; Jackson, D. D.; Haley, J., and Weakland, J. H. Toward a theory of schizophrenia. Behav. Sci., 1: 251-264, 1956.

36. Bateson, G., and Ruesch, J. Communication: The Social Matrix of Psychiatry. New York: Norton, 1951.

37. Bell, J. E. Family group therapy. Pub. Health Monogr. #64, 1961.

38. Bell, J. E. Recent advances in family group therapy. J. Child Psychol. Psychiat. 1: 1-15, 1962.

39. Bell, N.W., and Vogel, E.F. The emotionally disturbed child as the family scapegoat. In N.W. Bell and E.F. Vogel (Eds.), The Family. Glencoe, Ill.: Free Press, 1960.

40. Bell, N.W., and Vogel, E.F. (Eds.), The Family. Glencoe, Ill.: Free Press, 1960.

41. Berne, E. Transactional Analysis. New York: Grove Press, 1961.

42. Block, Jeanne; Patterson, V.; Block, J., and Jackson, D.D. A study of the parents of schizophrenic and neurotic children. Psychiatry, 21: 387-398, 1958.

43. Boszormenyi-Nagy, I. The concept of schizophrenia from the perspective of family treatment. Fam. Proc., 1: 103-113, 1962.

44. Bott, E. The Family and Social Network. London: Tavistock Publications, 1957.

45. Bowen, M. A family concept of schizophrenia. In D. D. Jackson (Ed.), The Etiology of Schizophrenia. New York: Basic Books, 1960.

46. Bowen, M.; Dysinger, R., and Basmania, B. Role of fathers in families with a schizophrenic patient. Amer. J. Psychiat., 115: 1017-1020, 1959.

47. Brady, J.P. Language in schizophrenia. Amer. J. Psychother., 12: 473-487, 1958.

48. Brodey, W.M. Some family operations of schizophrenia: a study of five hospitalized families each with a schizophrenic member. Arch. gen. Psychiat., 1: 379-402, 1959.

49. Brody, E.B. Social conflict and schizophrenic behavior in young adult Negro males. Psychiatry, 24: 337-346, 1961.

50. Brim, O.G. Family structure and sex-role learning by children. In N.W. Bell and E.F. Vogel (Eds.), The Family. Glencoe, Ill.: Free Press, 1960.

51. Brown, G.W. Experiences of discharged chronic schizophrenic patients in various types of living groups. Milbank Memorial Fund Quart., 37: 105-131, 1959.

52. Bruch, H. Studies in schizophrenia: psychotherapy with schizophrenics. Acta. Psychiat. Scand., 34, Suppl. 130: 28-48, 1959.

53. Bruch, H. Transformation of oral impulses in eating disorders: a conceptual approach. Psychiat. Quart., 35: 458-481, 1961.

54. Bruch, H., and Palombo, S. Conceptual problems in schizo-

phrenia. J. nerv. ment. Dis., 132: 114-117, 1961.
55. Bruch, H., and Rosenkotter, L. Psychotherapeutic aspects of teaching emotionally disturbed children. Psychiat. Quart., 34: 648-657, 1960.
56. Burton, A. The quest for the golden mean: a study in schizophrenia. In A. Burton (Ed.), Psychotherapy of the Psychoses. New York: Basic Books, 1960.
57. Burton, A. Schizophrenia and existence. Psychiatry, 23: 385-394, 1960.
58. Von Buddenbrook, W. The Senses. Ann Arbor: University of Michigan Press, Ann Arbor Science Paperbacks, 1958.
59. Calhoun, A.W. A Social History of the American Family. Cleveland: Arthur H. Clark Co., 1917.
60. Carroll, E.J. Treatment of the family as a unit. Penn. Med. J. 63: 57-62, 1960.
61. Carstairs, G., & Brown, G.W. A census of psychiatric cases in two contrasting communities. J. ment. Sci., 104: 72-81, 1958.
62. Chapman, L.J. Confusion of figurative and literal usages of words by schizophrenics and brain-damaged patients. J. abn. soc. Psychol., 60: 412-416, 1960.
63. Clausen, J.A., and Kohn, M.L. Social relations and schizophrenia; a research report and perspective. In D.D. Jackson (Ed. The Etiology of Schizophrenia. New York: Basic Books, 1960.
64. Cobb, S. Neurology. In S. Arieti (Ed.), American Handbook of Psychiatry. New York: Basic Books, 1959.
65. Cohen, R.A. The hospital as a therapeutic instrument. Psychiatry, 21: 29-35, 1958.
66. Coodley, A.E. Current aspects of delinquency and addiction. Arch. gen. Psychiat., 4: 632-640, 1961.
67. Cornelison, F.S. Review of C. Whitaker (Ed.), Psychotherapy of chronic schizophrenic patients. Psychosom. Med., 21: 84-85, 1959.
68. Coser, R.L. Laughter among colleagues. Psychiatry, 23: 81-95, 1960.
69. Curran, C.A. Counseling skills adapted to the learning of foreign languages. Bull. Menninger Clin., 25: 78-93, 1961.
70. Devereux, G. A sociological theory of schizophrenia. Psychoanal. Rev., 26: 315-342, 1939.
71. Devereux, G. The nature of the bizarre: a study of a schizophrenic's pseudo slip of the tongue. J. Hillside Hosp. 8: 266-278, 1959.
72. Dittmann, A.D., and Wynne, L.C. Linguistic techniques and the analysis of emotionality in interviews. J. abn. soc. Psychol., 63: 201-204, 1961.
73. Elkin, M. Short-contact counseling in a conciliation court. Soc. Casewk., 43: 184-190, 1962.
74. English, O.S. Clinical observations on direct analysis. In O.S. English, et al. (Eds.), Direct Analysis and Schizophrenia, Clinical Observations and Evaluations. New York: Grune & Stratton, 1961.
75. Erickson, M.H.; Haley, J., and Weakland, J.H. A transcript

of a trance induction with commentary. Amer. J. clin. Hypn. 2: 49-84, 1959.

76. Ferreira, A. J. The "double bind" and delinquent behavior. Arch. gen. Psychiat., 3: 359-367, 1960.

77. Ferreira, A. J. The semantics and the context of the schizophrenic's language. Arch. gen. Psychiat., 3: 128-138, 1960.

78. Fine, L. J. Nonverbal aspects of psychodrama. In J. M. Masserman and J. L. Moreno (Eds.), Progress in Psychotherapy. New York: Grune & Stratton, 1959.

79. Fisch, R. Home visits in a private psychiatric practice. Fam. Proc., 3: 114-126, 1964.

80. Fisch, R. Resistance to change in the psychiatric community. Arch. gen. Psychiat., 13: 359-366, 1965.

81. Fleck, S. Family dynamics and origin of schizophrenia. Psychosom. Med., 22: 333-344, 1960.

82. Fleck, S.; Norton, N.; Cornelison, A., and Lidz, T. The intrafamilial environment of the schizophrenic patient: II. Inter action between hospital staff and families. Psychiatry, 20: 343-350, 1957.

83. Flugel, J. C. The Psycho-Analytic Study of the Family. London: Hogarth Press, 1939.

84. Foote, N. N. Matching of husband and wife in phases of development. Reprint #7, Family Study Center, Univ. of Chicago, 1956.

85. Foudraine, J. Schizophrenia and the family, a survey of the literature 1956-1960 on the etiology of schizophrenia. Acta. Psychother. (Basel), 9: 82-110, 1961.

86. Framo, J. L. The theory of the technique of family treatment of schizophrenia. Fam. Proc., 1: 119-131, 1962.

87. Francisco, B. The theory behind the work done at the Mental Research Institute. Term paper presented at the School of Social Work, Berkeley, 1960.

88. Freud, A. The Ego and the Mechanisms of Defense. New York: Int. Univ. Press, 1960.

89. Friedman, A. S. Family therapy as conducted in the home. Fam. Proc., 1: 132-145, 1962.

90. Friedman, A. S., Boszormenyi-Nagy, I., Jurgels, J. E., Lincoln, Geraldine, Mitchell, H. E., Sonne, J. C., Speck, R. V., and Spivak, G. Psychotherapy for the Whole Family. New York: Springer Publishing Co., 1965.

91. Fromm, E. The Art of Loving. New York: Harper & Row, 1956.

92. Fry, W. F. The use of ataractic agents. Calif. Med., 98: 309-313, 1958.

93. Fry, W. F. Destructive behavior on hospital wards. Psychiat. Quart. Suppl., 33: 197-231, 1959.

94. Fry, W. F. The marital context of an anxiety syndrome. Fam. Proc., 1: 245-252, 1962.

95. Fry, W. F. The schizophrenogenic who? Psychoanal. psychoanal. Rev., 49: 68-73, 1962.

96. Fry, W. F. Sweet Madness: A Study of Humor. Palo Alto, Calif.: Pacific Books, 1963.

97. Fry, W. F., and Heersema, P. Conjoint family therapy: a new

dimension in psychotherapy. Topic. Prob. Psychother., 5:147-153, 1963.

98. Garmezy, N.; Clarke, A.R., and Stockner, C. Child rearing attitudes of mothers and fathers as reported by schizophrenic and normal parents. J. abn. soc. Psychol., 63: 178-182, 1961.

99. Greene, B.L. (Ed.) The Psychotherapies of Marital Disharmony New York: The Free Press, 1965.

100. Goffman, E. The Presentation of Self in Everyday Life. New York: Doubleday, Anchor Books, 1959.

101. Goldfarb, W. The mutual impact of mother and child in childhood schizophrenia. Amer. J. Orthopsychiat., 31:738-747, 1961.

102. Goodman, J.A. Social work services for alcoholics and their families. California's Health, Dec. 1, 1962.

103. Grotjahn, M. Trends in contemporary psychotherapy and the future of mental health. Brit. J. Med. Psychol., 33: 263-267, 1960.

104. Grunebaum, M.G. A study of learning problems of children: casework implications. Soc. Casewk., 42: 461-468, 1961.

105. Haley, J. Paradoxes in play, fantasy and psychotherapy. Psychiat. Res. Rep., 2: 52-58, 1955.

106. Haley, J. The art of psychoanalysis. ETC., 15: 190-200, 1958.

107. Haley, J. An interactional explanation of hypnosis. Amer. J. clin. Hypn., 1: 41-57, 1958.

108. Haley, J. Control in psychoanalytic psychotherapy. Progress in Psychotherapy, 4: 48-65, 1959.

109. Haley, J. The family of the schizophrenic: a model system. J. nerv. ment. Dis., 129: 357-374, 1959.

110. Haley, J. An interactional description of schizophrenia. Psychiatry, 22: 321-332, 1959.

111. Haley, J. Control of fear with hypnosis. Amer. J. clin. Hypn., 2: 109-115, 1960.

112. Haley, J. Observation of the family of the schizophrenic. Amer. J. Orthopsychiat., 30: 460-467, 1960.

113. Haley, J. Control in brief psychotherapy. Arch. gen. Psychiat., 4: 139-153, 1961.

114. Haley, J. Control in the psychotherapy of schizophrenics. Arch. gen. Psychiat., 5: 340-353, 1961.

115. Haley, J. Family experiments: a new type of experimentation. Fam. Proc., 1: 265-293, 1962.

116. Haley, J. Whither family therapy? Fam. Proc., 1: 69-103, 1962.

117. Haley, J. Marriage therapy. Arch. gen. Psychiat., 8: 213-234, 1963.

118. Haley, J. Strategies of Psychotherapy. New York: Grune & Stratton, 1963.

119. Haley, J., and Glick, I. Psychiatry and the Family: An Annotated Bibliography of Articles Published 1960-1964. Palo Alto: Fam. Process, 1965. (Order through Mental Research Institute, Palo Alto, California.)

120. Hall, E.T. The Silent Language. New York: Doubleday, 1959.

121. Handel, G. Psychological study of whole families. Psychol. Bull., 63: 19-41, 1965.

122. Handel, G. The Psychosocial Interior of the Family, Chicago: Aldine, 1967.

123. Harlow, H. F. The formation of learning sets. Psychol. Rev., 56: 51-65, 1949.

124. Hastings, D. W. Impotence and Frigidity. Boston: Little, Brown, 1963.

125. Hayakawa, S. I. The Use and Misuse of Language. Greenwich, Conn.: Fawcett Publications, Premier Books, 1962.

126. Hayakawa, S. I. Symbol, Status and Personality. New York: Harcourt, Brace & World, 1963.

127. Hayward, M. L. Schizophrenia and the "double bind." Psychiat. Quart., 34: 89-91, 1960.

128. Hess, R. D., and Handel, G. Family Worlds. Chicago: University of Chicago Press, 1959.

129. Hill, L. B. Psychotherapy of a schizophrenic. Amer. J. Psychoanal., 17: 99-109, 1957.

130. Hill, R. A critique of contemporary marriage and family research. Social Forces, 33: 268-277, 1955.

131. Hoffer, A., and Callbeck, M. J. Drug-induced schizophrenia. J. ment. Sci., 106: 138-159, 1960.

132. Hora, T. Epistemological aspects of existence and psychotherapy. J. indiv. Psychol., 15: 166-173, 1959.

133. Hora, T. Ontic perspectives in psychoanalysis. Amer. J. Psychother., 19: 134-142, 1959.

134. Hull, C. L.; Hovland, C. L.; Ross, R. T., et al. Mathematico-Deductive Theory of Rote Learning: A Study of Scientific Methodology. Yale University Press, 1940.

135. Huxley, A. The Art of Seeing. New York: Harper, 1942.

136. Jackson, D. D. An episode of sleepwalking. J. Amer. Psychoanal. Assn., 2: 503-508, 1954.

137. Jackson, D. D. Some factors influencing the Oedipus complex. Psychoanal. Quart., 23: 566-581, 1954.

138. Jackson, D. D. The therapist's personality in the psychotherapy of schizophrenics. Arch. Neurol. Psychiat., 74: 292-299, 1955.

139. Jackson, D. D. Countertransference and psychotherapy. In F. Fromm-Reichman and J. L. Moreno (Eds.), Progress in Psychotherapy. New York: Grune & Stratton, 1956.

140. Jackson, D. D. A note on the genesis of trauma in schizophrenia. Psychiatry, 20: 181-184, 1957.

141. Jackson, D. D. The psychiatrist in the medical clinic. Bull. Amer. Assn. Med. Clin., 6: 94-98, 1957.

142. Jackson, D. D. The question of family homeostasis. Psychiat. Quart. Suppl., 31: 79-90, 1957; first presented at APA, St. Louis, 1954.

143. Jackson, D. D. Theories of suicide. In E. Schneidman and N. Farberow (Eds.), Clues to Suicide. New York: McGraw-Hill, 1957.

144. Jackson, D. D. The family and sexuality. In C. Whitaker (Ed.),

The Psychotherapy of Chronic Schizophrenic Patients. Boston: Little, Brown, 1958.

145. Jackson, D. D. Guilt and the control of pleasure in schizoid personalities. Brit. J. med. Psychol., 31, Part 2: 124-130, 1958.

146. Jackson, D. D. Family interaction, family homeostasis, and some implications for conjoint family psychotherapy. In J. Masserman (Ed.), Individual and Familial Dynamics. New York: Grune & Stratton, 1959.

147. Jackson, D. D. The managing of acting out in a borderline personality. In A. Burton (Ed.), Case Studies in Counseling and Psychotherapy. New York: Prentice-Hall, 1959.

148. Jackson, D. D. (Ed.) The Etiology of Schizophrenia. New York: Basic Books, 1960.

149. Jackson, D. D. The monad, the dyad, and the family therapy of schizophrenics. In A. Burton (Ed.), Psychotherapy of Psychoses. New York: Basic Books, 1961.

150. Jackson, D. D. Action for mental illness — what kind? Stanford Med. Bull., 20: 77-80, 1962.

151. Jackson, D. D. Family therapy in the family of the schizophrenic. In M. I. Stein (Ed.), Contemporary Psychotherapies. Glencoe, Ill.: Free Press, 1962.

152. Jackson, D. D. Interactional psychotherapy. In M. I. Stein (Ed.), Contemporary Psychotherapies. Glencoe, Ill.: Free Press, 1962.

153. Jackson, D. D. Psychoanalytic education in the communication processes. In J. Masserman (Ed.), Science and Psychoanalysis New York: Grune & Stratton, 1962.

154. Jackson, D. D. The study of the family: Family rules. Fam. Proc. 12:589-594, 1965.

155. Jackson, D. D. Family rules: The marital quid pro quo. Arch. gen. Psychiat. 12: 589-594, 1965.

156. Jackson, D. D.; Block, J.; Block, Jeanne, and Patterson, V. Psychiatrists' conceptions of the schizophrenogenic parent. Arch. Neurol. Psychiat., 79: 448-458, 1958.

157. Jackson, D. D. and Haley, J. D. Transference revisited. J. nerv. ment. Dis., 137: 363-371, 1963.

158. Jackson, D. D.; Riskin, J., and Satir, V. M. A method of analysis of a family interview. Arch. gen. Psychiat., 5: 321-339, 1961.

159. Jackson, D. D., and Satir, V. M. Family diagnosis and family therapy. In N. Ackerman; F. L. Beatman, and S. N. Sherman (Eds.), Exploring the Base for Family Therapy. New York: Family Service Assn., 1961.

160. Jackson, D. D., and Watzlawick, P. The acute psychosis as a manifestation of growth experience. APA Res. Rep., 16: 83-94, 1963.

161. Jackson, D. D., and Weakland, J. H. Schizophrenic symptoms and family interaction. Arch. gen. Psychiat., 1: 618-621, 1959.

162. Jackson, D. D., and Weakland, J. H. Conjoint family therapy,

some considerations on theory, technique, and results. Psychiatry, 24, Suppl. to No. 2: 30-45, 1961.

163. Jackson, D. D. , and Yalom, I. Ulcerative colitis and family interaction. Arch. gen. Psychia. , 15: 410-418, 1966.

164. Jackson, D. D. , and Yalom, I. Family homeostasis and patient change. Curr. psychiat. Therapies, 4: 155-165, 1964.

165. Jaffe, J. Formal language patterns as defensive operations. In D. A. Barbara (Ed.), Psychological and Psychiatric Aspects of Speech and Hearing, Springfield, Ill. : Charles C. Thomas, 1960.

166. Jahoda, M. Current Concepts of Positive Mental Health. New York: Basic Books, 1960.

167. Johnson, A. ; Griffin, M. ; Watson, J. E. , and Beckett, P. Studies on schizophrenia: II. Observations on ego functions in schizophrenics. Psychiatry, 19: 143-148, 1956.

168. Kluckhohn, C. Variations in the human family. In N. W. Bell and E. F. Vogel (Eds.), The Family. Glencoe, Ill. : Free Press, 1960.

169. Kluckhohn, C. Mirror for Man. Greenwich, Conn. : Fawcett Publications, Premier Books, 1963.

170. Kohn, M. L. , and Clausen, J. A. Parental authority, behavior, and schizophrenia. Amer. J. Orthopsychiat. , 26: 297-313, 1956.

171. Kohn, M. L. , and Clausen, J. A. Social isolation and schizophrenia. Amer. Sociol. Rev. , 20: 265-273, 1955.

172. Krasner, L. The use of generalized reinforcers in psychotherapy research. Psychol. Rep. , 1: 19-25, 1955.

173. Laing, R. D. The Self and Others, Further Studies in Sanity and Madness. London: Tavistock Publ. , 1961.

174. Laird, C. The Miracle of Language. Greenwich, Conn. : Fawcett Publications, Premier Books, 1963.

175. Leder, H. H. Acculturation and the "double bind. " M. A. Thesis, Dept. of Anthropology, Stanford University, 1959.

176. Lewis, O. The Children of Sanchez: Autobiography of a Mexican Family. New York: Random House, 1961.

177. Lichtenberg, J. D. , and Pao, Ping-Nie. The prognostic and therapeutic significance of the husband-wife relationship for hospitalized schizophrenic women. Psychiatry, 23: 209-213, 1960.

178. Lidz, T. Schizophrenia and the family. Psychiatry, 21: 21-27, 1958.

179. Lidz, T. ; Cornelison, A. ; Fleck, S. , and Terry, D. The intrafamilial environment of the schizophrenic patient: I. The father. Psychiatry, 20: 329-342, 1957.

180. Lidz, T. ; Cornelison, A. ; Fleck, S. , and Terry, D. The intrafamilial environment of schizophrenic patients: II. Marital schism and marital skew. Amer. J. Psychiat. , 114: 241-248, 1957.

181. Lidz, T. : Cornelison, A. ; Fleck, S. , and Terry, D. The intrafamilial environment of the schizophrenic patient: IV. Parental personalities and family interaction. Amer. J. Orthopsychiat. , 28: 764-776, 1958.

182. Lidz, T.; Cornelison, A.; Fleck, S., and Terry, D. The intrafamilial environment of the schizophrenic patient: VI. Transmission of irrationality. Arch. Neurol. Psychiat., 79: 305-316, 1958.

183. Lidz, T.; Parker, B., and Cornelison, A. The role of the father in the family environment of the schizophrenic patient. Amer. J. Psychiat., 113: 126-132, 1956.

184. Loch, W. Anmerkungen zur pathogenese und metapsychologie einer schizophrenen psychose. Psyche (Berl.), 15: 684-720, 1961.

185. Lu, Y. C. Contradictory parental expectations in schizophrenia. Arch. gen. Psychiat., 6: 219-234, 1962.

186. MacGregor, R., Ritchie, A. M., Serrano, A. C., Schuster, F. P., McDonald, E. C., and Goolishan, H. A. Multiple Impact Therapy with Families. New York: McGraw-Hill, 1964.

187. Mednik, S. A. A learning theory approach to research in schizophrenia. Psychol. Bull., 55: 316-327, 1958.

188. Meissner, W. W. Thinking about the family: psychiatric aspects. Fam. Proc., 3: 1-40, 1964.

189. Meyers, D. I., and Goldfarb, W. Studies of perplexity in mothers of schizophrenic children. Amer. J. Orthopsychiat., 31: 551-564, 1961.

190. Minuchin, S. Conflict-resolution family therapy. Amer. J. Orthopsychiat., 28: 278-286, 1965.

191. Montagu, A. Man In Process. Cleveland: World Pub. Co., 1961.

192. Mora, G. Recent American psychiatric developments (since 1939). In S. Arieti (Ed.), American Handbook of Psychiatry. New York: Basic Books, 1959.

193. McReynolds, P. Anxiety, perception, and schizophrenia. In D. D. Jackson (Ed.), The Etiology of Schizophrenia. New York: Basic Books, 1960.

194. Novey, S. The outpatient treatment of borderline paranoid states. Psychiatry, 23: 357-364, 1960.

195. Offenkrantz, W., and Rechschaffen, A. Clinical studies of sequential dreams. Arch. gen. Psychiat., 8: 497-508, 1963.

196. Ostow, M. Discussion of Arieti's "Recent conceptions and misconceptions of schizophrenia." Amer. J. Psychother., 14: 23-29, 1960.

197. Otto, H. A. The family resource development program: the production of criteria for assessing family strengths. Fam. Proc., 2: 329-339, 1963.

198. Parker, E. The Seven Ages of Women. Baltimore: Johns Hopkins Press, 1960.

199. Parloff, M. B. The family in psychotherapy. Arch. gen. Psychiat., 4: 445-451, 1961.

200. Pemberton, W. H. Nondirective reorientation in counseling. ETC, 16: 407-416, 1959.

201. Penrose, L. S. Mental illness in husband and wife: a contribution to the study of associative mating. Psychiat. Quart. Suppl., 18: 161-166, 1944.

202. Perls, F. S. The Gestalt Therapy. New York: Julian Press, 1951.

203. Perls, F. Ego Hunger and Aggression. Big Sur, Calif.: Esalen Institute, 1966.

204. Perr, H. M. Criteria distinguishing parents of schizophrenic and normal children. Arch. Neurol. Psychiat., 79: 217-224, 1958.

205. Pollak, O. Some conceptual steps toward a theoretical framework for studying family situations and child development. Children, 4: 169-173, 1957.

206. Pollak, O. The midwest seminar on family diagnosis and treatment. Soc. Casewk., 42: 319-324, 1961.

207. Query, J. M. N. Pre-morbid adjustment and family structure: a comparison of selected rural and urban men. J. nerv. ment. Dis., 133: 333-338, 1961.

208. Rashkis, H. A., and Singer, R. D. The psychology of schizophrenia. Arch. gen. Psychiat., 1: 406-416, 1959.

209. Rieman, D. W. Health department nursing services for mentally ill patients and their families. Nursing Outlook, 10: 450-452, 1962.

210. Rioch, D. McK. The sense and the noise. Psychiatry, 24, Suppl. to No. 2: 7-18, 1961.

211. Riskin, J. Methodology for studying family interaction. Arch. gen. Psychiat., 8: 343-348, 1963.

212. Robinson, M. N. The Power of Sexual Surrender. New York: New American Library, Signet Books, 1962.

213. Rosenbaum, C. P. Patient-family similarities in schizophrenia. Arch. gen. Psychiat., 5: 120-126, 1961.

214. Rosenthal, D. Confusion of identity and the frequency of schizophrenia in twins. Arch. gen. Psychiat., 3: 297-304, 1960.

215. Rowan, M., and Pannor, R. Work with teen-age unwed parents and their families. Child Welfare, Dec. 1959.

216. Ruesch, J. General theory of communication in psychiatry. In S. Arieti (Ed.), American Handbook of Psychiatry. New York: Basic Books, 1959.

217. Ruesch, J. Therapeutic Communication. New York: Norton, 1961.

218. Ruesch, J., and Bateson, G. Communication: the Social Matrix of Society. New York: Norton, 1951.

219. Ryckoff, I. M.; Day, J., and Wynne, L. C. Maintenance of stereotyped roles in families of schizophrenics. Arch. gen. Psychiat., 1: 93-98, 1959.

220. Sanua, V. D. Sociocultural factors in families of schizophrenics: a review of the literature. Psychiatry, 24: 246-265, 1961.

221. Sapirstein, M. R. Paradoxes of Everyday Life. Greenwich, Conn.: Fawcett Publications, Premier Books, 1963.

222. Satir, V. M. The quest for survival. Acta Psychother., (Basel), 2: 33-38, 1963.

223. Satir, V. M. Schizophrenia and family therapy. In Social Work Practice, 1963, published for the National Conference on So-

cial Welfare, Columbus, Ohio. New York: Columbia Univ. Press, 1963.

224. Satir, Virginia M. The family as a treatment unit. Confina Psychiatrica, 8: 37-42, 1965.

225. Savage, C. Countertransference in the therapy of schizophrenics. Psychiatry, 24: 53-60, 1961.

226. Scheflen, A. E. Regressive one-to-one relationships. Psychiat. Quart., 34: 692-709, 1960.

227. Scheflen, A. E. A Psychotherapy of Schizophrenia: Direct Analysis. Springfield, Ill.: Thomas, 1961.

228. Schwartz, D. P. The integrative effect of participation. Psychiatry, 22: 81-86, 1962.

229. Scott, J. P. Critical periods in behavioral development. Science, 138: 949-957, 1962.

230. Searles, H. F. Positive feelings in the relationship between the schizophrenic and his mother. Int. J. Psycho-Anal., 39: 569-586, 1958.

231. Searles, H. F. The effort to drive the other person crazy—an element in the aetiology and psychotherapy of schizophrenia. Brit. J. med. Psychol., 32: 1-18, 1959.

232. Searles, H. F. Integration and differentiation in schizophrenia: an overall view. Brit. J. med. Psychol., 32: 261-281, 1959.

233. Silverman, M., and Silverman, Margaret. Psychiatry inside the family circle. Saturday Evening Post, July 28, 1962.

234. Singer, R. D. Organization as a unifying concept in schizophrenia. Arch. gen. Psychiat., 2: 61-74, 1960.

235. Smith, J. H. The metaphor of the manic-depressive. Psychiatry, 23: 375-383, 1960.

236. Sommer, R. Visitors to the mental hospitals. Ment. Hygiene, 40: 8-15, 1959.

237. Spiegel, J. P. New perspectives in the study of the family. Marr. & Fam. Living, 16: 4-12, 1954.

238. Spiegel, J. P. Homeostatic mechanisms within the family. In I. Galdston (Ed.), The Family in Contemporary Society. New York: Int. Univ. Press, 1958.

239. Spiegel, J. P. The resolution of role conflict within the family. In N. W. Bell and E. F. Vogel (Eds.), The Family. Glencoe, Ill.: Free Press, 1960.

240. Spiegel, J. P., and Bell, N. W. The family of the psychiatric patient. In S. Arieti (Ed.), American Handbook of Psychiatry. New York: Basic Books, 1959.

241. Stanton, A. H., and Schwartz, M. S. The Mental Hospital. New York: Basic Books, 1954.

242. Stierlin, H. The adaptation to the "stronger" person's reality, some aspects of the symbiotic relationship of the schizophrenic. Psychiatry, 22: 143-152, 1959.

243. Stierlin, H. Report on the Hawaiian divisional meeting of the APA, May 1958. Psyche (Berl.), 13: 843-845, 1959/60.

244. Sullivan, H. S. The onset of schizophrenia. Amer. J. Psychiat., 7: 105-134, 1927.

245. Sullivan, H. S. Introduction to the study of interpersonal relations. Psychiatry, 1: 121-134, 1938.
246. Symonds, A. Discussion of Arieti's recent conceptions and misconceptions of schizophrenia. Amer. J. Psychother., 14: 21-23, 1960.
247. Szasz, T. S. The Myth of Mental Illness, Foundations of a Theory of Personal Conduct. New York: Hoeber-Harper, 1961.
248. Szurek, S., and Boatman, M. A clinical study of childhood schizophrenia. In D. D. Jackson (Ed.), The Etiology of Schizophrenia. New York: Basic Books, 1960.
249. Titchener, J., and Emerson, R. Some methods for the study of family interaction in personality development. Psychiat. Res. Rep. No. 10: 72-8, 1958.
250. U. S. Department of Health, Education and Welfare. Family Therapy: A Selected Annotated Bibliography. Bethesda, Md.: Public Health Service, National Institutes of Health, 1965.
251. Urquhart, R., and Forrest, A. D. Clinical trial of promazine hydrochloride and acetylpromazine in chronic schizophrenic patients. J. ment. Sci., 105: 260-264, 1959.
252. Varley, B. K. "Reaching out" therapy with schizophrenic patients. Amer. J. Orthopsychiat., 29: 407-416, 1959.
253. Watts, A. W. Nature, Man and Woman. New York: Pantheon Books, 1958.
254. Watts, A. W. Psychotherapy East and West. New York: Pantheon Books, 1961.
255. Watzlawick, P. A review of the double bind theory. Fam. Proc. 2: 132-153, 1963.
256. Watzlawick, P. An Anthology of Human Communication. Palo Alto, Calif.: Science and Behavior Books, 1963.
257. Watzlawick, P. A structured family interview. Fam. Proc., 5: 256-271, 1966.
258. Watzlawick, P., Beavin, J., and Jackson, D. Pragmatics of Human Communication. New York: W. W. Norton, 1967.
259. Weakland, J. The "double bind" hypothesis of schizophrenia and three-party interaction. In D. D. Jackson (Ed.), The Etiology of Schizophrenia. New York: Basic Books, 1960.
260. Weakland, J. H. The essence of anthropological education. Amer. Anthrop., 63: 1094-1097, 1961.
261. Weakland, J. H. Review of Coercive Persuasion by E. H. Schein, I. Schnier, and C. H. Barker. J. Asian Studies, 21: 84-86, 1961.
262. Weakland, J. H. Family therapy as a research arena. Fam. Proc., 1: 63-68, 1962.
263. Weakland, J. H., and Fry, W. F. Letters of mothers of schizophrenics. Amer. J. Orthopsychiat., 32: 604-623, 1962.
264. Weakland, J. H., and Jackson, D. D. Patient and therapist observations on the circumstances of a schizophrenic episode. Arch. Neurol. Psychiat., 79: 554-574, 1958.
265. Weigert, E. Loneliness and trust — basic factors of human existence. Psychiatry, 23: 121-131, 1960.
266. White, R. B. The mother-conflict in Schreber's Psychosis. Int. J. Psycho-Anal., 42: 55-73, 1961.

267. Will, O.A. Human relatedness and the schizophrenic reaction. Psychiatry, 22: 205-223, 1959.
268. Winder, C.L. Some psychological studies of schizophrenia. In D.D. Jackson (Ed.), The Etiology of Schizophrenia. New York: Basic Books, 1960.
269. Wolman, B.B. The fathers of schizophrenic patients. Acta. Psychother., (Basel), 9: 193-210, 1961.
270. Wynne, L.C.: Ryckoff, I.M.; Day, J., and Hirsch, S.I. Pseudo mutuality in family relationships of schizophrenics. Psychiatry, 21: 205-220, 1958.
271. Zuk, G., and Boszormenyi-Nagy, I. Family Therapy and Disturbed Families. Palo Alto: Science and Behavior Books, 1967.

Index

Science and Behavior Books is in the process of preparing and distributing some exciting and dramatic new audio and videotapes by Virginia Satir. For information on the tapes and a free brochure write to Post Office Box 11457, Palo Alto, California 94306.

Preliminary Comments about video-tapes offered in the brochure:

" 'Family in Crisis' is one of the most moving episodes of a therapist in action with a family that it has been my privilege to see."

Ben N. Ard, Jr., Ph.D.
Professor of Counseling
San Francisco State College

"The Family Reconstruction which follows 'Family in Crisis' by Virginia Satir demonstrates beyond a doubt her superb understanding of the family process as well as her ability to communicate her findings with perception and a great deal of humor."

DeWitt Baldwin, M.D.
Professor of Psychiatry
University of Nevada

"The six tapes Virginia Satir did at the University of Winnipeg (the Canadian Tapes) are beautiful examples of a perceptive and gifted family therapist treating actual families. No one could view these tapes without being deeply affected emotionally."

Robert S. Spitzer, M.D.
Former Director, Family Project
Mental Research Institute
Palo Alto, California

Science and Behavior Books
Post Office Box 11457
Palo Alto, CA 94306